WAVERLEY ABB

INSI

CHILD AND ADULT BULLYING

Helena Wilkinson

CWR

WAVERLEY ABBEY INSIGHT SERIES

The *Waverley Abbey Insight Series* has been developed in response to the great need to help people understand and face some key issues that many of us struggle with today. CWR's ministry spans teaching, training and publishing, and this series draws on all of these areas of ministry.

Sourced from material first presented over Insight Days by CWR at either Waverley Abbey House or Pilgrim Hall, presenters and authors have worked in close co-operation to bring this series together, offering clear insight, teaching and help on a broad range of subjects and issues. Bringing biblical understanding and godly insight, these books are written both for those who help others and those who face these issues themselves.

Published 2013 by CWR, Waverley Abbey House, Waverley Lane, Farnham, Surrey GU9 8EP UK. Registered Charity No. 294387. Registered Limited Company No. 1990308.

The right of Helena Wilkinson to be identified as the author of this work has been asserted by her in accordance with the Copyright, Designs and Patents Act 1988, sections 77 and 78.

For list of National Distributors visit www.cwr.org.uk/distributors

Unless otherwise indicated, all Scripture references are from the Holy Bible: New International Version (NIV), copyright © 1973, 1978, 1984 by the International Bible Society. Other translations used: Amplified: The Amplified Bible Scripture taken from the THE AMPLIFIED BIBLE, Old Testament copyright © 1965, 1987 by the Zondervan Corporation. The Amplified New Testament copyright © 1958, 1987 by the Lockman Foundation. Used by permission. NLT: Scripture quotations marked NLT are taken from the *Holy Bible*, New Living Translation, copyright © 1996, 2004. Used by permission of Tyndale House Publishers, Inc., Wheaton, Illinois 60189. All rights reserved.

Concept development, editing, design and production by CWR
Printed in England by Linney Group
ISBN: 978-1-85345-912-2

CONTENTS

Dedication

In my research I have come across some amazing people whose lives were once shattered by the disempowerment and long-term consequences of bullying. Their contributions have given me a wider perspective of the depth and complexities involved and I dedicate this book to them in honour of the rebuilding of their broken lives.

Thanks

My grateful thanks go to Nikki Cole, who has endless patience and much skill in pulling apart my writing and challenging me to see beyond my initial limited view.

Disclaimer

Whilst I hold qualifications in counselling I do not claim to be an expert in the field of bullying. My insights come from personal experience, research and interviews with targets of bullying. The information given is accurate to the best of my knowledge.

Other books by Helena Wilkinson

Puppet on a String (Horsham: RoperPenberthy Publishing, 2004); *Snakes & Ladders* (Horsham: RoperPenberthy Publishing, 2007); *Beyond Chaotic Eating* (Horsham: RoperPenberthy Publishing, 2001); *Beyond Singleness* (Horsham: RoperPenberthy Publishing, 2007); *A Way out of Despair* (Farnham: CWR, 1995); *Breaking Free from Loneliness* (Horsham: RoperPenberthy Publishing, 2004); *Insight into Eating Disorders* (Farnham: CWR, 2006); *Inspiring Women – Finding Freedom*, (Farnham: CWR, 2007); *Designed for Living*, Jeannette Barwick and Helena Wilkinson (Farnham: CWR, 2009). Available through Amazon. Titles published by CWR can also be ordered from www.cwr.org.uk/store

INTRODUCTION

Bullying in the UK is reaching epidemic proportions. It is said that 69% of children are bullied at school.[1] Bullying is a very real problem for a large number of people at work too[2] and many have been bullied within relationships and in other contexts. However, most would struggle to admit to themselves that they are being, or have been, bullied, let alone tell anyone.

Being bullied is a nightmare from which you long to wake. Your mind races as it revisits the distorted words, incriminating comments and unjust actions of the bully. Anxiety soars in anticipation of what's going to happen next and feelings of powerlessness overwhelm.

For many years if I heard the word 'bullying' I would be transported to my convent boarding school where, as a quivering ten-year-old, I endured emotional torment and physical punishment on a regular basis. Bullying in the day ate into my self-confidence and stirred up feelings of not being liked, wanted or valued. Bullying at night was the worst because I knew that no one would ever see or suspect what was happening.

Overwhelmed by feelings of isolation, and having been told not to tell or I'd die, I'd lie awake, staring out of the little window opposite my bed. My heart was aching for connection with someone who cared and I longed for a way out of the web of silent suffering. My tear-filled eyes would scan the night sky and be drawn to the bright light of the moon which offered a glimmer of hope. I'd seen the historic landing of Neil Armstrong and team when I was about five years old and in my naivety I thought there was still a man on the moon.

'It's happened again,' I'd whisper.

Of course I never received a response, but somehow that didn't matter. Just knowing someone was listening (or so I thought) was a great source of comfort.

Being bullied as a child put me in a vulnerable position as an adult. Time and again I would find myself sucked into the manipulation and control of other people, causing no end of complications. It took me considerable time to realise that these traumatic encounters, even with people deemed as 'safe', were, in fact, bullying in a different guise.

In my work (largely with people with eating disorders) I began to notice a similar pattern: the person traumatised as a child and not helped to deal with their vulnerability becomes an easy target for repeated adult bullying. My personal and professional experiences led to a passion to write a book addressing *both* childhood and adulthood bullying that would empower people to grow in courage, strength and skill. You may not always find it comfortable reading this book, but I encourage you to persevere. If you, yourself, have been a target of bullying, I believe that by the end you will have gained, amongst other things, hope and strength to face bullying and to heal from its effects. If you are a friend, family member, helper or counsellor, I believe the insights you gain will help the target to take courage and face the issues, and will enable you to journey together towards healing.

Helena Wilkinson
Gower, Swansea 2012

CHAPTER 1

ALL SHAPES AND SIZES

Half the population are bullied ... most people only realise it when
they read this page.

Tim Field[1]

SPOTTING THE TARGET

Some years ago, whilst on a speaking tour in Zimbabwe, I was
watching a group of sun-scorched elephants churning up the
earth and graciously dropping the much sought-after trace
elements into their mouths. In a split second the tranquility of
the early morning African wilderness was rudely interrupted by
a large vulture swooping down at great speed, forcibly snatching
the bacon from my plate and leaving me rather stunned. Bullying
is not dissimilar: the bully has their eye on a target, swoops in,
attacks and leaves the person reeling.

Sometimes the attack is less obvious but equally damaging.
Rather than acting with force, an unassuming bird craftily
sidles up to a little sea creature and persistently pecks away at

its shell. The tapping of the sharp beak eventually cracks the outside, leaving the tender inside raw and exposed; in the same way the bully consistently undermines the target, who becomes a shadow of their former self.

SOWING SEEDS OF DOUBT

Most bullies are either unaware of the impact of their behaviour or extremely clever at disguising it. Either way, seeds of doubt are sown in the target's mind, leaving the confused individual asking themselves: 'Am I really being bullied or is it just me?' Perhaps you've asked that very same question or wondered what it is about you that leads to your being intimidated by others.

The doubt in your own mind is bad enough, but to prove to others that you are being bullied is harder still. It's frequently one person's word against another with few, if any, witnesses. Like sand slipping between your fingers, the evidence of the existence of bullying quickly disappears and you are left with nothing tangible to explain. Bullying all too easily becomes the target's best kept secret, maybe for years.

AM I BEING BULLIED?

Perhaps you are wondering about your own experiences, in which case consider the list below. If your answer is 'yes' to most of the questions, it's likely that bullying is taking/has taken place.

With reference to a particular person, do you ...
- Experience high levels of anxiety in their presence?
- Find yourself subjected to hurtful actions or words over and over again?

- Find that your words and actions are often misrepresented or even twisted?
- Feel treated differently from others?
- Feel you have to please in order to stay in their 'good books'/ avoid anger or criticism?
- Make excuses to avoid coming into contact?
- Suffer from self-doubt/loss of confidence which has worsened since knowing them?
- Find attempting to confront them results in further humiliation?
- Frequently feel inadequate, out of control and experience a sense of shame?
- Wonder if their inconsistent, harmful actions are intentional?
- Find you are blamed for someone else's mistakes?

It's OK to admit you are being bullied ...
Admitting to being bullied, however long ago, is OK. Acceptance is the first step to recovery.

See yourself as a target and not a victim ...
The word 'target' puts the onus on the other person's actions against you; the word 'victim' puts the onus on your feelings of helplessness. As Dave Chapman, creator of www.kickbully.com says 'You may be a target of bullying, but you don't have to become a victim'.[2]

Not alone ...
If you are being bullied or have been bullied, you are certainly not alone. It's surprising the number of people who have been carrying the bullying wound for many years.

WHAT IS BULLYING?

Bullying is not the occasional burst of anger, unkind word or thoughtless action; it is persistent intimidation, criticism, control, manipulation and misuse of power. However cleverly it is disguised, and sometimes it is well hidden behind a façade of care, *bullying is abuse.*

It is said that, 'Bullying is the wilful, conscious desire to hurt another and put him/her under stress'.[3] Whilst this is largely true, some bullies act out of unresolved personal issues and learned behaviour rather than making a calculated decision to harm. Carried out with malice or not, bullying consists of an *imbalance* of power: one stronger character clearly having the 'upper hand' over someone less able to defend themselves.

Wherever it occurs – school, work, home, hospital, prison, Armed Forces, social setting or place of worship – bullying leaves behind a devastating imprint, physically and psychologically. Its cruel legacies include: a body hammered by stress and a mind dominated by depression, lack of self-belief, feelings of isolation and thoughts of suicide. Fear, anxiety, guilt, shame, sadness, grief, frustration and anger all play their part in the daily life of the person victimised by the persecutory actions of the bully. As Carl W. Buechner rightfully points out regarding the actions of the bully: 'They [target] may forget what you [bully] said, but they will never forget how you made them feel.'[4]

Bullying cuts across gender, social class, intellect and talent. For some it has shattered their lives and destroyed their ability to work; for others it has contributed to their determination to succeed. Many who have found fame have experienced bullying, including: Kate Winslet, *actress;* Tessa Sanderson, *athlete;* Joe Calzaghe, *boxer;* Lady Gaga, *singer;* Jodie Marsh, *glamour girl, body builder.*

TYPES OF BULLYING

Bullying comes in all shapes and sizes but is essentially physical or psychological.

PHYSICAL BULLYING

Boys automatically come to mind when people talk about physical bullying, and men are more likely than women to use aggression in relationships. But don't be fooled into thinking that physical bullying is exclusively male. My own experience as a child included acts of physical harm, where I was stabbed with compass ends, kicked in the stomach and had my head pushed into the wall. My friend, Mary, who was in the same dormitory, still carries physical consequences as a result of being kicked in the bladder many times and forbidden from going to the toilet.

Physical bullying, which also includes threatening to act in these ways, includes someone repeatedly:

- Hitting you
- Pushing you over
- Tripping you up
- Pulling your hair
- Harming your body in some way
- Being sexually abusive
- Hiding or stealing your possessions
- Ruining your belongings

Take note

If you are being physically bullied, don't think it will just 'go away'; it rarely does. Get help! (see Useful Resources, p.135.)

PSYCHOLOGICAL BULLYING

We all know the childhood saying, 'Sticks and stones may break my bones but words will never hurt me' – the fact is it's *not true*. Words *can* and *do* inflict more pain than the biggest stick or the heaviest stone. Words have energy and power. *What* we say, *how* we say it, *what we mean by it* – these all affect us and other people. Equally powerful are the silent treatment and the disapproving looks of the bully, which can slice a person in two and strip them of their dignity in seconds.

PAUSE FOR THOUGHT ...

What words spoken to you have felt like an arrow shooting through your heart and have resulted in self-doubt? Remember: just because negative words are spoken doesn't mean that they are true. Try to imagine a shield of protection around you so that the words don't continue to embed.

The bully uses a variety of methods to intimidate.

CONTROL

When you are being controlled, you live with the feeling that you are the puppet with someone else pulling the strings. Driven by the need to be 'top dog', bullies isolate their targets, boosting their own sense of value, and try to:
• Take over
• Define who you are and what you are like
• Tell you what to do or how to do it
• Give the impression that you can't do without them
• Make out that they are the ones who know best
• Demand that change be on their terms

- Blame their anger on you

MANIPULATION

Manipulation is when someone tries to influence or control another for their own purposes. Bullies manipulate through both their words and their actions. They:
- Turn statements around so that you come out looking bad
- Say one thing and later say that they didn't
- Play on your emotions to get what they want
- Try to 'mould you' to become compliant
- Make you feel that you owe them a favour
- Use threats and blame, trying to make you feel guilty
- Misrepresent you to others
- Refuse to take responsibility for their own actions

EXCLUSION

Exclusion is the act of excluding, shutting out or keeping apart. Both child and adult bullies use it to exert power with the message: *'You're* not a part of the pack', resulting in feelings of rejection. Even animals respond negatively to exclusion – shut a dog behind a door or turn your back on him and he whines. The emotional impact of exclusion for both animals and humans is huge.

Child bullies ...
- Send you to 'Coventry' (They don't talk to you and encourage others to do the same.)
- Leave you out and ignore you

Adult bullies ...
- Treat you in a similar way to child bullies

13

- Cut you out of the communication loop
- Fail to include you in relevant meetings at work
- Prevent you from being involved in appropriate decision-making processes
- Talk *about you* rather than *to you*
- Talk to others in your presence whilst ignoring you
- Intentionally leave you out or fail to invite you to social gatherings

PAUSE FOR THOUGHT ...

Who has excluded you? Have you drawn negative conclusions about yourself as a result? I encourage you to spend a few moments reminding yourself of your worth. Remember that exclusion says more about the other person than about you.

HUMILIATION

Humiliation is being made to appear foolish in front of others. Bullies use it to disgrace, belittle, ridicule, disempower and push their targets down the 'pecking order'. When you are humiliated you feel deprived of rights and you lose all sense of dignity.

Child bullies love to laugh at their targets, taunt them and show them up in front of their friends, telling tales and pointing out vulnerabilities. Carrie was humiliated at school:

> When I was about fourteen, the girls I so desperately wanted to be friends with used to humiliate me by putting grass in my lunch and making me eat it in front of the class. They said I was a cow so had to eat the grass. If I refused, then they would corner me in the toilets later and push the sandwich into my mouth.

In addition to 'up-front humiliation' adults also act in more devious ways, drawing their targets aside to avoid revealing their behaviour to those around. Their derogatory words and hypocritical actions rob the person of their reputation and self-respect, leaving them feeling disgraced.

Bullies ...
- Dismiss, discount or silence what you have to say
- Withhold acknowledgement and deny recognition
- Make you wait unnecessarily
- Reduce your authority, responsibility, role etc
- Falsely accuse you in front of others
- Ridicule you, give you dirty looks or make you look stupid
- Use intimidation or threats to reduce your safety or security

CRITICISM
Criticism can be both constructive and destructive. Constructive criticism has the motive of helping you to grow; destructive criticism points out mistakes in a negative manner and is a destroyer of self-esteem.

The bully uses criticism to chip away at the target, weakening the person's self-belief through persistent nitpicking, blaming, fault-finding, sarcasm and patronising comments, alongside non-verbal cues of disapproval. Confidence is eroded and vulnerability increased as the bully speaks ill of the person – maligning, gossiping and pointing the finger. The bully influences others to do the same, causing the target to feel that there is something profoundly wrong with them, and making it impossible for the person to defend themselves without further criticism.

Perhaps some of the following comments ring true for you:

'Don't you *ever* listen?'; 'I can't rely on you for anything'; 'I didn't expect much from you'; 'If it wasn't for you it would've been all right'; 'It would have been quicker if I'd done it myself'.

If you are still being bullied ...
Try to keep a written record of names, dates, incidents, who else was around and whether other people have ever mentioned that they have been treated wrongly by the same person. It can be a useful means of proving that bullying has occurred and working out whether there is a pattern to the bullying.

REFLECTION
Bullying is never OK. Perhaps you have been bullied and have not been able to talk with anyone about what it really felt like; or maybe you have minimised what happened. People often need to be given permission to own the experience of bullying and long to talk about their experience without a sense of being judged.

ACTION
If you have been bullied, try to write down on a piece of paper the names of the people who harmed you and what they did. It only needs to be a few words or the odd sentence. Fold the paper over, so that you don't have to look at it for the time being, and tuck it into the back of the book. (We'll talk later about what to do with it.)

PRAYER
I invite you to pray with me:
Dear God, I don't quite know how I feel about everything that's happened. Thinking about bullying fills me with fear, but I'm going to take one step at a time and I ask You to help me. Amen.

CHAPTER 2

CHILDHOOD BULLYING

The bitterest part of being bullied is the memory that you were once happy.

Perry Morgan[1]

BULLYING AT SCHOOL

When the word 'bullying' is used we all tend to think of school bullying. Most of us will have experienced degrees of it. Fortunately for the majority it was short-lived and not too destructive. However, for some, the bullying was malicious, ongoing and soul-destroying, resulting in lasting psychological damage.

Schools are the hot seat of name-calling, insults, cruel jokes, disapproving looks, gossip, vindictive actions, exclusion, sexual innuendos and physical cruelty. The grounds, cafeterias, toilets, classrooms, halls, corridors and dormitories are all common places of attack and the journey to school by public transport has a magnetic pull for the school bully. Outside school, streets, alleys and parks all are favoured spots for shaming an innocent target.

Who gets targeted?

The child-target may be physically smaller or younger, with the tendency to display a degree of insecurity. New children are often picked on and, of course, for some reason there are children that just don't seem to be liked. Bullies will go to incredible lengths to find an excuse to taunt that person: having a disability or disfiguration, being on the autistic spectrum, being highly sensitive, coming from a different cultural or social background, not wearing designer gear, not having the right phone, being fat, being the teacher's pet etc. A child who is socially less popular is a prime target for bullying; but given that much childhood bullying is also driven by jealousy and envy, the child who has integrity and is hard-working is also vulnerable.

Whatever the initial reason, once the bully has latched on to the target they rarely let go until they cease to get a reaction. If the original reason for bullying the child changes (an overweight child loses weight, for example) the bully may find another reason to target the child. More often it is the fear and anxiety shown by the child-target (rather than the 'excuse' for targeting the child) that give the child-bully the incentive to keep going.

PAUSE FOR THOUGHT ...

What do you think might have contributed to *you* being victimised? Remember that even if there was something about you that attracted bullies, *bullying is not your fault and bullying is never acceptable.*

HELPLESSNESS AND WORTHLESSNESS

The victimised child feels helpless and worthless, convincing themselves that there's something wrong with them. To add insult to injury other children may side with, or appear to side with, the bully. The reason for this is that deep down they fear that by not doing so they put themselves potentially in the firing line. The already ostracised target ends up feeling 'disliked' not only by the bully but by others – perhaps even by children they thought were friends. To the distraught child, and even many onlookers, it can appear that the bully is popular when, in reality, the 'friendships' are probably out of fear rather than choice. The sense of being an outsider and the feelings of loneliness can be crippling.

Whatever the nature of the bullying it has catastrophic effects. The child-target is particularly susceptible to psychological damage, due to not having the same resources and ability to reason as an adult. The period of childhood and adolescence is an important time in the shaping of identity and the building of confidence and relationships; bullying can quite literally savage the building blocks of a person's life.

The damage can continue to affect the person throughout adulthood, especially if the bullying has been severe and sustained. Nearly all the people with whom I have spoken in the course of writing this book said that their confidence, self-perception and trust in people are still affected. A high percentage also admitted that in adulthood they now find themselves overreacting to situations of personal injustice, such as being treated differently, and they find it hard to fit in.

INDICATORS OF BULLYING

Children who are being bullied are unlikely to immediately confide in an adult. Some never tell. Therefore, it's important for anyone connected with children to keep an eye out for potential signs.

Signs of bullying ...
- Change in mood or personality
- Change in eating habits – under or over eating
- Withdrawal, depression, secrecy
- School phobia or truancy
- Lowered grades or failure to concentrate
- Increased fear and anxiety
- Unexplained bruises, scratches, cuts
- Coming home with missing possessions or money
- Not wanting to walk or take the bus to school
- Nightmares or difficulty in sleeping
- Self-loathing and loss of confidence and self-esteem

TEACHERS AND BULLYING

Besides bullying each other, teachers can bully children, and vice versa. The experience of being bullied by a teacher is deeply wounding, slicing into the very heart and confidence of the child, not least because children look to teachers for guidance and as role models. The reasons why teachers bully vary. I was bullied by one particular teacher when I was in my mid-teens. My disability and vulnerability obviously pressed buttons in her and my passivity angered her. It would seem that some of her unresolved personal issues were channelled in her 'put downs' and dismissal of me. I remember being tormented by thoughts that there was something profoundly wrong with me and I could never do anything right.

One reason children are bullied by teachers is because they are gifted; the bullying being born out of jealousy and the teacher's resentment of lack of opportunities to pursue their aspirations. An exceptionally able child being targeted is sometimes referred to as the 'poppy head syndrome': a teacher feels the need to 'cut down' a gifted child to bring him or her to the level of the others. Sarcasm, running pupils down, being negative and dismissive are all tactics used. One girl described her experience at music college: she was humiliated in front of the class, shouted at in 'one-to-one' tuition, and the teacher walked out on her. It came to a head one day when the teacher told her that she was wasting everyone's time and should give up. The girl took the teacher at her word and did just that. It took twenty years for her to gain sufficient confidence to contemplate teaching music.

CYBERBULLYING

As more and more young people rely on computers, the internet and mobile phones, the electronic age has introduced a new form of bullying, commonly known as 'cyberbullying'. This can take on a frightening life of its own, destroying the reputation of an individual and causing no end of trouble. Text messages, emails, chat rooms, blogs, instant messaging and social networks are all vehicles used to undermine and attack.

The cyberbully takes advantage of the accessibility of technology, spreading demeaning rumours, telling lies, inventing stories, intimidating, posing threats and even encouraging others to join in the mockery. Cybertechnology enables the bully to carry out the onslaught at any time of day or night, taking bullying right into the target's home and creating the oppressive feeling of there being no means of escape. Pictures, video and comments can be posted not just for a whole school but the entire internet community to see, thus furthering the humiliation.

As children get older, the insults may move from childish 'put downs' to derogatory comments which are often sexual in nature.

Detailed information (true or not) of dates or promiscuous activity may be plastered on the internet, causing the young person to become not only a laughing stock but vulnerable to predators.

Parents may be unaware of the current sites used by their children and the oppression they experience when accessing destructive social media and texts. Children are often afraid to tell their parents for fear that their computer or phone could be taken away which, for many people these days, is like having their right arm cut off.

Cyberbullying can take different forms:[2]

- *Flaming*. Online fights using electronic messages with angry and vulgar language.
- *Harassment*. Repeatedly sending nasty, mean, and insulting messages.
- *Denigration*. 'Dissing' someone online. Sending or posting gossip or rumours about a person to damage his or her reputation or friendships.
- *Impersonation*. Pretending to be someone else and sending or posting material to get that person in trouble or danger or to damage that person's reputation or friendships.
- *Outing*. Sharing someone's secrets or embarrassing information or images online.
- *Trickery*. Talking someone into revealing secrets or embarrassing information, then sharing it online.
- *Exclusion*. Intentionally and cruelly excluding someone from an online group.
- *Cyberstalking*. Repeated, intense harassment and denigration that includes threats or creates significant fear.

BULLYING IN THE HOME

Home is supposed to be a safe place, but sadly for some it is far from such. Siblings, parents, grandparents and other relatives have all played their part in bullying and abusing family members. Being harmed by 'loved ones' only exacerbates the confusion over what constitutes love and increases the crippling self-doubt of the target.

Examples of adult relatives bullying children ...

- Physically harming a child or enforcing rules with a heavy hand
- Humiliating and instilling fear in a child
- Belittling or insulting in private and public
- Being overbearing or seeking to control the child's life
- Making negative remarks about preferences and abilities
- Employing constant sarcasm and criticism
- Shouting, threatening and name-calling
- Telling the child that they are not wanted or shouldn't have been born
- Competing with a child or setting up competitiveness between siblings
- Violating a child's privacy

Parents who don't have good parenting skills often use aggression and manipulation. Whilst it might appear to solve the short-term problem of controlling children, it not only causes difficulties in childhood but can hamper the child's ability to handle the adult world in a healthy way. A bullying parental style often results in the child having two options:

1. To act as a victim (which may include being manipulative, because that's what the child has been forced into).
2. To be aggressive/abusive (because that's what has been role-modelled).

Neither of these increases the chances of a happy and fulfilling life.

Jenny, now in her fifties, was bullied at school and at home. She said that the feeling she felt most when relating to her mum was one of 'being wrong'.

> I went through emotional and physical abuse much of my childhood. If my ideas were different from my mum's she ridiculed me and at times lashed out physically. I remember on one occasion asking my mum if she'd play 'Cowboys and Indians'. She tied me up and left me sitting on a slab of concrete by the outside toilet for four hours. She then said it served me right for expecting her to play.

SIBLINGS AND BULLYING

The story of Joseph and his brothers is a good example of bullying between siblings. It is taken from the Bible, but is known by many as the well-acclaimed musical *Joseph and The Amazing Technicolor Dreamcoat*. Joseph was the favourite son of Jacob. His eleven brothers resented the fact that their father doted on him and they were infuriated by Jacob giving Joseph a special coat. Joseph also had incredible dreams which he claimed predicted that he would be far more successful than any of his brothers. The brothers were unbelievably jealous and decided to take action. They planned to throw Joseph into a pit to die, but at the last minute changed their minds and sold him as a slave in return for cash. They tore his coat, covered it in goat's blood and told their father that Joseph was dead. Through extraordinary circumstances (orchestrated by God) Joseph became an advisor to Pharaoh (the Egyptian king) and ended up wealthy and successful. His brothers, in contrast, suffered terrible famine in their land and travelled to Egypt in search of food. There they met Joseph; although at first they didn't recognise him. Joseph tested their honesty before he finally revealed his true identity, thus reuniting the family (see Genesis 45). As the story of Joseph illustrates, the outcome for those who are bullied does not have to be negative.

Bullying from a sibling is far more than sibling rivalry, where two equals compete and 'fight' with each other. The sibling who is being bullied tends to be degraded, ostracised, belittled, controlled, excluded and made to feel inferior or even defective.

As the number of 'blended' families increases, children across a broad age range, with different backgrounds, often live together in the same household. This creates power differentials and insecurities which can set the scene for bullying. There may be more opportunities for tension, loss, pain, feelings of displacement and competition between siblings, all looking for attention and acceptance. If this isn't handled well or the parents are too wrapped up in their new relationship, bullying can escalate.

WHAT YOU CAN DO

If you are or have been experiencing bullying, or equally are trying to help a child who is currently being bullied, it's important to do something to stop it and to deal with the effects, even if difficult.

If you are a young person being bullied ...
- Talk to an adult you can trust
- Try to stay calm, look confident and, if possible, walk away
- Take part in activities that will boost your self-esteem and confidence, such as joining a club
- Phone ChildLine (0800 1111) or visit www.bullying.co.uk for advice and support

If it's cyberbullying, then as well as the ideas above ...
- Keep a record of what has been posted and show it to a trusted adult
- Ask for your school's 'safe internet use' policy
- Find out how to block someone from access to your phone/ social network sites etc.

If you are a parent of a child being bullied ...
- Try not to ignore the situation or overreact, however difficult this may be
- If possible, read the school's anti-bullying policy and talk to your child about bullying
- If it's sibling bullying, try to address the underlying causes (eg jealousy) in a calm way, understanding both children and affirming the positives
- If it's cyberbullying, endeavour to learn more about the technology and communication networks your child uses
- Ask your child to show you any nasty messages they receive
- Make sure that you and your child realise that the more personal information is given out via instant messaging and blogs or online journals, the more it can be used against them
- If your child finds it hard to talk about 'bad things happening',

devise a way in which this will be communicated, such as writing you a letter and leaving it in a particular place
- Encourage your child never to respond to abusive messages
- For further suggestions see: http://kiwicommons.com/index.php?p=12004&tag=what-can-parents-do-when-their-childteen-is-being-bullied-or-cyberbullied

REFLECTION

Remind yourself that there is no shame in still suffering from the effects of bullying. It does not make you less of a person, but simply says that the wounds were deep and are in need of healing.

ACTION

In what way do your childhood experiences affect you now? If you have not sought help or you have done so in the past but you still find yourself struggling, why not look into having some counselling/prayer ministry (see Useful Resources, p.135).

PRAYER

I invite you to pray with me:

Dear God, sometimes I find myself reacting out of the pain of my childhood bullying and the pain is deep. Jesus, You understand what it is like to be mocked and treated badly. I ask You to show me where the wounds are … words and actions which need to be healed … and to come and heal those areas. Amen.

CHAPTER 3

WORKPLACE BULLYING

> I believe bullying is the main, but least recognised, cause of stress in the workplace today.
>
> Tim Field[1]

UNREASONABLE BEHAVIOUR

The BBC News Online once published an article[2], asking the question: 'What do soldiers under fire and bullied workers have in common?' The reporter went on to answer the question by saying: '"Not much"' you may think. However research from a leading psychologist, Dr Tehrani, suggests: "The symptoms displayed by people who have been in conflict situations and workplaces where bullying happens are strikingly similar. Both groups suffer nightmares, are jumpy and seem fuelled by too much adrenaline."'

In essence, the article describes both sets of people as 'battle scarred'. Someone bullied in the workplace explained it this way: 'I feel as if I spent years in a war zone where my confidence was thoroughly stripped and I've been left fearful and wondering what's going to happen next. I'm constantly waiting for the attack and I feel shaky a lot of the time, despite the fact that I'm no longer being bullied.'

Workplace bullying is an insidious problem and can be difficult to identify. Those who bully often operate in an inconspicuous or seemingly harmless way but actually with grave effect. It's a hard challenge because bullies create a culture of fear and intimidation that discourages employees from asserting themselves. It's equally difficult for targets to recognise, certainly initially, that the treatment they have been enduring is, in fact, bullying. People who are bullied in the workplace often feel in a double bind: to say nothing results in ongoing bullying, yet to speak out runs the risk of job loss. Some targets describe a web of conspiracy: when they try to challenge what has been happening it results in people 'closing rank' to protect the organisation.

If you are wondering whether you have been bullied in the workplace, consider the list below.

I feel …
- As if I'm on an emotional rollercoaster
- Threatened, humiliated and vulnerable
- Anxious and frustrated far more than I used to
- Confused and insecure in the presence of the other person
- As if I keep hitting a brick wall
- Fearful of interactions with the other person
- Misunderstood and misrepresented
- Powerless to solve problems for fear of the other person retaliating

- As if my thoughts and feelings are discounted
- Criticised and put down
- Supported one day and undermined the next

ACAS (Advisory, Conciliation and Arbitration Service) which aims to improve organisations and working life through better employment relations states: 'Everyone should be treated with dignity and respect at work.'[3] Sadly, they're not and it has been said that 'workplace bullying has become a silent epidemic'.[4]

WHAT IS WORKPLACE BULLYING?

Workplace bullying is far more than a bit of aggro from a 'tough boss' or a 'difficult colleague'. It is a set of behaviours emanating from an individual which cause both stress and distress. In the workplace a certain amount of pressure or 'being pushed' is beneficial, coaxing people out of complacency and enabling them to reach their potential. Bullying, on the other hand, does not help people to reach their potential but 'pushes them over the edge'.

Andy Ellis from Ruskin College, Oxford, explains how degrees of stress can help us to perform better, whereas an overload of stress (as with bullying) is highly destructive physically and emotionally.

The chart below shows how stress in the early stages can 'rev up' the body and enhance performance in the workplace, thus the term 'I perform better under pressure'. If this condition is allowed to go unchecked however and the body is revved up further then performance will ultimately decline and the person's health will degenerate as demonstrated in fig 1.[5]

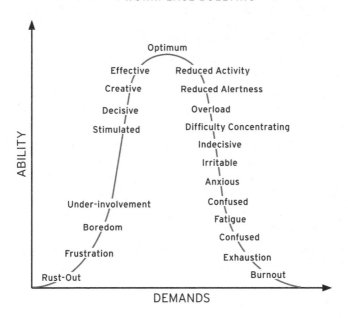

Fig 1

Bullying shows itself through both actions and attitudes which are destructive to the target, often affecting both work performance and mental health.

The bully's actions (some but not all may be present)
- Micromanages and criticises your work
- Bullies instead of dealing with conflict and change
- Causes confusion – may act as a friend and at other times bully you
- Spreads malicious rumours and gossips about you
- Uses confidential information about you to your detriment

- Generates an unmanageable workload
- Seems intent on controlling your behaviour against your will
- Denies you information and fails to communicate adequately
- Shifts blame and makes you a scapegoat
- Increases responsibility without sufficient back-up or accountability
- Prevents you from progressing, by blocking promotion or training opportunities
- Encourages others to turn against you or sows seeds of doubt in them
- Takes away areas of responsibility without good reason
- Sets unrealistic tasks and deadlines, leading to failure
- Makes unwelcome sexual advances – touching, standing too close, display of offensive materials, asking for sexual favours

The bully's attitudes (again some but not all may be present)
- Belittles, embarrasses, intimidates, humiliates or shouts
- Is persistently offensive, abusive and intimidating
- Doesn't want to know about any interpersonal, work or safety issues
- Is overbearing and misuses power and authority
- Ignores, ostracises, excludes or isolates you
- Ridicules you in front of others
- Resists any attempt to have a normal, mutually respectful working relationship
- Is constantly fault-finding and nit-picking
- Is divisive, for example, saying one thing to one person and something else to another
- Is dismissive, especially if his/her actions are questioned

PAUSE FOR THOUGHT ...

What aspects of the bullies in your life have most affected you? Try to separate yourself from their words and actions and to see yourself casting the actions away from you.

Some bullies may appear to act differently in different work contexts – a behaviour that is particularly insidious. When relating to a group of colleagues or staff (if the bully is the manager), the bully may appear very reasonable. Then when alone together the bully may treat the target despicably, as Dave Chapman points out:[6]

> Initially the bully may provide the target with a sense of belonging, the feeling of being an integral part of the team and praise and promises may be lavished on the target. However, the bully is insincere and the underlying intention is to exploit the target's emotions.
>
> When the target sees through the bully's manipulations and begins to resist the control, there are suggestions that others don't think very highly of the target. The basic message is that if the target doesn't do as the bully wants then the target is failing both the boss and peers.
>
> If the target continues to resist, the bully switches tactics, causing the target to feel fear, guilt, shame, jealously or hate. There is, of course, the enticement that relief from painful emotions, and return to positive ones, await. All the target needs to do is to submit to the bully's dominance.

Some people successfully challenge the bully; others don't challenge because of the tactics we have just explored. It's not easy when one is dealing with a person whose style of relating is probably interwoven with an inability to face reality, the tendency to cover up problems and the need to be right.

TYPES OF BULLIES

Bill Eddy, an attorney, therapist, mediator and the President of the High Conflict Institute believes that bullies at work are High Conflict People ('HCPs') with high conflict personalities. He suggests that they bring this behaviour with them rather than either the bully reacting to an external issue or other people making them behave in this way. Effectively he is saying that bullying is part of 'who they are' – driven by their lifelong pattern of thinking, feeling and behaving, which existed prior to taking on this particular job.

He goes on to say that, from his observations, there are four personality types most often engaged in workplace bullying. Each of these types is trying to overcome a sense of weakness or fear in themselves, although they are usually unaware of this. (And don't try to point it out to them!) They are unconsciously driven to find and attack what he calls their 'Targets of Blame', because being able to hurt others helps them briefly to feel less anxious and helpless themselves. (Once again they may be totally unaware of what they are doing.) Their target can be anyone. It's not personal. It's about the bully, not about the target.

'I'm Very Superior' type

These bullies are stuck trying to prove to themselves and others that they are superior beings. They are really afraid of being seen as inferior, but this fear is not conscious and they will become very defensive if you suggest that they are worried about being seen as inferior. They show frequent disdain and disrespect towards those closest to them. This is mostly verbal, but they may engage in humiliating jokes, tricks or maneuvers to make you look bad (to make them look good, they hope). This is automatic behaviour for them.

34

'Love-You, Hate-You' type

These bullies often seek revenge for perceived rejections from those they thought were very good friends. Once their fantasy of friendship fades, they retaliate. Even if you did nothing, they don't check out misinformation – instead they act on it. They may spread rumours and make claims that you are an extremely uncaring or unethical person. If there was a conflict, they want others to believe that it's all your fault. They have a lot of all-or-nothing thinking and they jump to conclusions. 'You're with me or you're against me.' They can easily fly into a rage, and sometimes become violent or stalk their targets.

'I Need to Dominate' type

These bullies go beyond just wanting to appear superior. They enjoy hurting other people. They fear being dominated, so they try to find someone, somewhere, who they can dominate. As long as they are harming someone else, they feel less vulnerable. They may say hurtful things, but they often do hurtful things, including stealing from those they are closest to, manipulating you into doing favours and then stabbing you in the back, and being willing to destroy your career for some short-term goal. You may feel that you are being manipulated or in danger. Be sceptical of strange schemes. They are con artists.

'I Can't Trust Anyone' type
These bullies are highly suspicious of others and may believe that you are taking advantage of them, when you don't even know them personally. They bear a grudge and will attack you before (they think) you are going to attack them. They can spread rumors that you want to harm them, and they believe it themselves. They often create high conflict situations because of their excessive fears of everyone else.

All these bullies feel that they are victims. They think that you are a danger to them, and so they believe they are justified in attacking you. While it may seem that they are enjoying bullying others, it is not true enjoyment. They enjoy the momentary feeling of being in power. Most people don't need to have power over someone else in a negative way. But, for these bullies, that is the only satisfaction in a daily struggle of feeling that they are everyone else's victim. Remember, this feeling is not conscious and you will make it worse if you suggest this to them.[7]

Bullying by managers
Anyone within a workplace can be a bully but when the bully is your manager there is a real sense of being trapped. 'Strong management can unfortunately sometimes tip over into bullying behaviour. A culture where employees are consulted and problems discussed is less likely to encourage bullying and harassment than one where there is an authoritarian management style.'[8] Tim Field outlines the difference between a manager and a bully in the chart below.[9]

Manager	Bully
Decisive	Random, impulsive
Accepts responsibility	Abdicates responsibility
Shares credit	Plagiarises, takes all the credit
Acknowledges failings	Denies failings, always blames others
Consistent	Inconsistent
Fair, treats all equally	Shows favouritism
Respectful and considerate	Disrespectful and inconsiderate
Values others	Constantly devalues others
Includes everyone	Includes and excludes people selectively
Leads by example	Dominates, sets a poor example
Truthful	Economical, uses distortion/fabrication
Confident	Insecure, arrogant
Behaviourally mature	Behaviourally immature
Cares about staff, the business etc	Cares only about self
Gets on well with people	Identifies only with clones of self
Assertive	Aggressive
Delegates	Dumps
Builds team spirit	Divisive, uses manipulation and threat
Uses influencing skills	Alienates, divides, creates fear and uncertainty
Motivates	Demotivates
Listens, guides, instructs	Tells
Shares information freely	Withholds information, uses it as a weapon
Always strives for clarity	Revels in confusion, divide and rule etc
Trusts people to get on with the job	Interferes, dictates and controls
Has honesty and integrity	Exhibits hypocrisy and duplicity

TACKLING THE PROBLEM

With such potentially destructive actions taking place at work, how does anyone protect themselves from being bullied? Some organisations work hard to prevent bullying and set in place a procedure for dealing with it. They may provide a staff handbook as a way of communicating with employees how they define bullying and what colleagues are to do if they find themselves in such a situation. In the future, you may want to ask what the organisational policies on bullying are.

Steps to consider

Every case of workplace bullying is different. How you handle bullying will depend on your work environment, the nature of the bullying and what, if any, procedures exist at your workplace. The following tips may be helpful:

- Don't take it personally. Try to avoid becoming self-critical. Remember, bullying behaviour is about the bully, not about you.
- Keep a record of bullying: place, date, time, persons (both those involved and those present) and what was said or done.
- Keep an ear out for anyone else who may have also experienced bullying in the organisation and look to see if there is a pattern to the bullying.
- Try to be methodical and unemotional. Remember that being emotional will attract a bully.
- Don't allow yourself to become isolated. Bullies endeavour to alienate targets, so make the effort to speak with people and avoid being alone with the bully.
- Be aware of how you come across. A fearful and negative attitude will exacerbate the problem. If possible try to take

your feelings about the bullying outside the office and stay focused and positive in the office.

- Be careful how much personal information you share: information about your life gives the bully power.
- When the bullying occurs, try to distract the bully by picking something up which needs to be looked at or mentioning someone who needs to be called. If it becomes very difficult, give a valid reason to leave the room, but do not make a hasty retreat.
- Check whether your employer has a policy and a complaint resolution procedure for workplace bullying.
- Seek advice from your human resources officer, union official, grievance officer or whoever is responsible for staff welfare.
- If the person who has been bullying you is involved in the complaint procedure, then consider seeking outside advice, for example, from the Citizens Advice Bureau.
- If you are aware of others who are being bullied, try to make a joint complaint.
- Some workplaces offer a counselling service, which you may find useful in building life skills for dealing with bullying and overcoming its effects. Alternatively you can seek outside counselling.

REFLECTION

Some would argue that the boss or colleague whom you describe as a bully is simply a 'strong character', 'just getting their job done' or 'a bit dictatorial, but basically OK'. Workplace bullies are more than these!

ACTION

Write down the characteristics you admire in managers/colleagues. Now write down the characteristics you see in the person who is/has been bullying you. No doubt there are big discrepancies.

PRAYER

I invite you to pray with me:

Dear God, I can see more and more the wrong actions and attitudes which have taken place at work. I don't want to harbour bitterness in my heart but I need to admit the ways in which I have been hurt. Please help me to face the truth and find release from the damage. Amen.

CHAPTER 4

RELATIONSHIP BULLYING

All forms of abuse follow a pattern that, left unchecked, will only increase over time.

Beth J. Lueders[1]

DESTRUCTIVE RELATIONSHIPS

We should feel protected and safe in romantic relationships. There are many reasons why people don't, including bullying. Maybe you are one of those people who has been, or still is, caught up in an unstable relationship, even if you have never labelled your partner as a bully. As painful as it is, I hope that this chapter may help to explain a little more what constitutes relationship bullying and what to do to help yourself or someone you care about. We will largely focus on emotional, rather than physical, bullying in relationships. Physical bullying is, in most cases, described as domestic violence. In my opinion, this is a subject best dealt with in a book of its own. Should you be caught in such a situation, I urge you to seek help (**National Domestic Violence Helpline 0808 2000 247**).

RECOGNISING THE SIGNS

In the context of relationships, bullying is persistent behaviour which degrades and undermines, destroying your soul and killing your ability to love. Bullying in relationships is often harder to admit than in other situations: love easily covers abusive actions, minimising its effects and putting you in a position of denial.

Some people mistake intensity for love and they fall into the trap of feeling that 'the good times in the relationship are worth the bad treatment'. Intense emotions prevent you thinking clearly and cloud your judgment. It's important to see the destructiveness of the relationship, because only then can you decide what to do. If you feel as though you have to walk on eggshells – constantly watching what you say and do in order to avoid a blow-up – the chances are that your relationship is abusive. The signs listed below will help to clarify whether the relationship is unhealthy.

How you feel
- On edge because you are never sure how your partner is going to behave
- You must avoid certain topics out of fear of angering your partner
- It's as if you can't do anything right
- Your 'buttons are pushed' on purpose
- You don't feel good about yourself
- It's as if you are going crazy at times
- Emotionally numb or helpless
- You are often trying to meet your partner's demands
- Your partner doesn't 'hear' you

- You often have to work out how to behave so as not to 'upset' your partner
- Your words are twisted and communication misunderstood
- Emotionally blackmailed
- Insecure much of the time
- Judged

How your partner behaves
- Quickly changes from kind and caring to angry, loud, critical or judgmental
- Is unpredictable
- Humiliates and shames you
- Criticises you and puts you down
- Is sarcastic, cynical and critical
- Dismisses your opinions
- Blames you for their unacceptable behaviour
- Is possessive and overly jealous
- Controls where you go, what you do and access to finances etc
- Restricts your involvement with friends
- Has hurt you, or threatened to hurt you
- Demands love, affection, care, intimacy on their terms
- Tends to 'filter' what you say
- Offers inconsistent support
- Is inflexible and insists that their way is *the only way*

People to whom I spoke about relationship bullying said that they often had a sense that something wasn't right and a feeling of unease. However, they covered it up for the sake of a peaceful marriage or relationship to avoid conflicts within the family.

CYCLE OF ABUSE

The 'cycle of abuse' is a social cycle theory developed by Lenore Walker in the 1970s, originally known as the 'cycle of violence'.[2] It explains the sequence of behaviour that takes place in an abusive relationship. Perhaps it looks familiar? The cycle follows four phases, which will be repeated until the conflict stops.

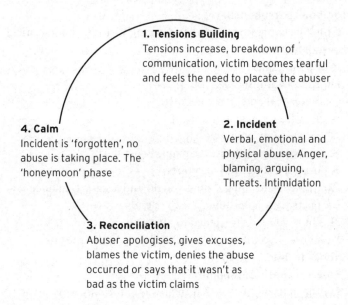

1. Tensions Building
Tensions increase, breakdown of communication, victim becomes tearful and feels the need to placate the abuser

2. Incident
Verbal, emotional and physical abuse. Anger, blaming, arguing. Threats. Intimidation

3. Reconciliation
Abuser apologises, gives excuses, blames the victim, denies the abuse occurred or says that it wasn't as bad as the victim claims

4. Calm
Incident is 'forgotten', no abuse is taking place. The 'honeymoon' phase

Claire's first husband was a bully but she found it hard to accept this for a long time because of the 'good' times they would have together. She explains:

John was a very gregarious guy – life and soul of the party – and it was this that drew me to him in the first place – his charisma, humour and the fact that he attracted people. However, at home he was also very controlling and had angry outbursts. We were very different personalities and quite often had differing opinions. John always had to be right and if I contradicted him in any way (ie stated a different opinion) he became verbally very strong and intimidating and sometimes threw things. He would put me down and crush me. It would escalate into hours, sometimes days, of pointing the finger at me and my faults (often taken out of context). I came away feeling as if I'd committed the unforgivable sin. I'd be reduced to tears and feel badly shaken up. Visitors, work or something else would cause a shift in the dynamic. A more normal life would return and he might even apologise. My hopes would rise and we'd go back to a reasonably good relationship. Then, BANG, it would happen all over again and I would be trembling.

PAUSE FOR THOUGHT ...

When you try to communicate with the other person do they dominate and you struggle to say how you feel? When needing to talk through 'issues' try the 'one person speaking at a time' rule (one person holds an object and talks uninterrupted and vice versa).

HEALTHY RELATIONSHIPS

To understand what unhealthy behaviour is within a relationship, it is useful to consider the components of a healthy relationship:

- Being emotionally affirming and understanding
- Listening to each other in a non-judgmental way
- Valuing both your and your partner's opinions
- Respecting your partner's rights to their own feelings
- Accepting responsibility for yourself and letting your partner take responsibility for him/herself
- Admitting being wrong when it is appropriate
- Communicating openly and truthfully, acknowledging hurtful words and actions
- Talking and acting in such a way that you both feel safe/comfortable

On the subject of relationships, the Bible speaks of how we are to strive for the very best for the other person and to show care, concern and respect. The apostle Paul, in his letter to the Colossians, says to husbands (although the same applies to wives, girlfriends and boyfriends, no doubt): 'Husbands, love your wives [be affectionate and sympathetic with them] and do not be harsh *or* bitter *or* resentful toward them' (Col. 3:19, *Amplified*). Hostility, maligning, criticism and the causing of intentional pain should not be a part of relationships.

The Greek word for love in this passage is *agapao*, which means to love, value, esteem, feel or manifest generous concern for, be faithful towards, to delight in, to set store upon.[3] In other words, to love another is to treat them like they are the most wonderful and amazing person in the world.

WHAT TO DO

As hard as it is to accept, none of us can change another individual, but we can change ourselves and the way we react, which should improve the situation.

Consider the following:

1. Hold on to self-respect. You will need to affirm yourself if your partner is not doing so. Focus on your strengths and qualities. What do other people say are your gifts, abilities and positive aspects of your personality? Write them down and read them regularly.

2. Make a conscious effort to look after yourself. When someone doesn't treat you well, it's all too easy to neglect yourself. Looking after yourself may include:

a) Finding a place of safety if you are being physically hurt

b) Making sure that you eat properly, exercise, rest and take care of your appearance

c) Looking at what you need in order to reduce stress levels

d) Doing something that you really enjoy each week.

3. When your partner treats you well, tell them that you appreciate them, so that you are affirming positive actions and attitudes.

4. Use 'I statements' not 'You statements'. For example: 'When this happens I feel ...' rather than 'When this happens you make me feel ...'. 'You statements' lead to defensive reactions and accusations.

5. Don't make excuses for your partner. At the start of any relationship, we all tend to be blind to the faults and inconsistencies of the other person: we see them through rose-tinted glasses. Within abusive relationships sometimes the

target finds it hard to face the reality of the wrong actions of their partner. If things are going to change it's vital to see the abusive nature of the relationship.

6. Don't be blackmailed. Being blackmailed shows itself through words such as:

a) 'You'll never find anyone else to love you like I do'

b) 'Without me, you're nothing'

c) 'It was your fault I acted the way I did'

7. Don't try to cope alone. There are excellent agencies that are able to help, as well as many good counsellors and supportive churches (see Useful Resources, p.135).

REFLECTION

Conflict and bullying in relationships can so easily result in feelings of being trapped. Is this how you feel or perhaps felt when you were in a difficult relationship in the past?

ACTION

Endeavour to take one day at a time and look at what you can do *today*, rather than panic about the situation never ending. We cannot necessarily change the other person, but we can change ourselves, which has a knock-on effect. What can you do differently today?

PRAYER

I invite you to pray with me:

Dear God, I feel such pain. I wish it could just go away. I ask You to show me ways in which I can change my reactions so that my partner reacts differently too. Please intervene. Amen.

CHAPTER 5

SPIRITUAL BULLYING

Abusive churches, past and present, are first and foremost characterized by strong, control-oriented leadership.

R. Euroth[1]

MISUSE OF POWER

Sadly, Christian and other religious establishments are not exempt from bullying, although spiritual bullying, most commonly known as spiritual abuse, is arguably less recognised and researched than other forms of bullying. 'It is all too common that people in positions of spiritual authority use their positions to disempower and manipulate others, rather than to support them and build them up'[2]

Bullying in a place that is meant to be underpinned by love has the potential to not only damage the individual but also to disintegrate their faith: many people have lost their faith and been put off places of worship because of their experiences.

Definitions of spiritual abuse include:
- 'The mistreatment of a person who is in need of help, support or greater spiritual empowerment, with the result of weakening, undermining or decreasing that person's spiritual empowerment'.[3]
- 'Someone using their power within a framework of spiritual belief or practice to satisfy their needs at the expense of others.'[4]

Spiritual abuse is commonly associated with cults and all too often isn't sufficiently recognised as occurring in churches, Christian organisations and other places of worship. Those on the receiving end feel misunderstood. It is most likely that they do not receive adequate help to recover from its devastating consequences.

Signs to look out for:
- Manipulation, dominance and control
- The belief that the minister/leader always knows best
- A lack of accountability within the church/organisation – spoken about but rarely carried out
- Pride, arrogance and lack of admitting to mistakes amongst leaders
- Members feel unable to ask questions or raise issues without being seen as the problem
- Defensive responses from leaders to theological discussion or queries about the organisation
- Unspoken rules: you don't know what they are until you've broken them
- Undermining, devaluing or cutting the person off because of theological differences

- Threats or undermining of members if they mention leaving the church/organisation
- The minister/leader becoming angry or unpleasant when challenged
- Emphasis on external image, placing its importance above individuals
- Elitism – 'There is no other church/organisation like this'
- Increasing expectation of commitment
- Social isolation of members from individuals outside the church
- Secrecy – over finance, decisions etc
- Overemphasis on money
- Misuse of Scripture
- Workers within the church/organisation being given enormous amounts of responsibility but no authority
- Emotional reaction from leaders seems disproportionate to the event(s) members report[5]

Anyone may become a bully but leaders, by virtue of their position, often get away with bullying. They tend to be seen as always right and hence their misuse of authority is not always spotted until the damage has begun.

In Christian and other faith organisations if the leader's management and people skills are limited, you may find that they use bullying tactics rather than healthy directing of others. In these circumstances the leaders fail to guide, confront change or deal with conflict appropriately and tend to favour those who are in agreement with them or are a part of their 'network'.

HARMING THE WOUNDED

Churches and faith organisations often attract people who are hurting and are seeking solace, comfort, healing and direction, in a safe place. Unfortunately the help given is not always beneficial and in some cases constitutes bullying. When suffering from emotional or physical problems, people may find themselves being 'helped' by someone who, through intention or naivety, acts in ways that are controlling and abusive, further harming the already vulnerable individual. This often involves a judgmental, narrow-minded, intimidating or dismissive approach. The prophet Jeremiah talked about those who heal other people's wounds superficially: 'They offer superficial treatments for my people's mortal wound' (Jer. 8:11, NLT).

Destructive approaches include:
- Oversimplifying complex problems
- Overspiritualising and not considering other factors, such as physical and emotional causes
- Telling the person that they lack faith
- Telling the person that they wouldn't feel anxious if they knew their identity in Christ
- Making strong statements such as: 'Christians shouldn't suffer from depression'
- Applying Scripture without understanding the problem
- Stating: 'What I just said may sound harsh, but God wants to teach you something'
- Making someone face issues before they are ready
- Using shame/false guilt to reinforce what they are saying to the individual

PAUSE FOR THOUGHT ...

What has been said to you that, rather than helping, has wounded you further? Remember that even those in authority do not always encourage. Whatever is said and done should never contradict Scripture.

WHAT THE BIBLE SAYS

The Bible says a lot about the misuse of power which, in effect, is bullying. The books of Ezekiel and Jeremiah are classic examples: God was angered by the fact that the leaders were not using their authority appropriately (Ezek. 13:10; Jer. 6:13).

In the New Testament, Jesus warned people about the legalistic, judgmental Pharisees. They sound rather similar to the way we have described bullies, don't they? He spoke of them as 'whitewashed tombs' (Matt. 23:27). At that time people held onto a belief that if you touched a tomb you would be defiled. Jesus is effectively warning them that if they came under the influence of the Pharisees they could become defiled – affected spiritually. In the same way, if we come under the influence of a bully, it affects us not just emotionally but spiritually too.

Jesus draws the analogy of spiritually abusive leaders as 'vicious wolves' – people who devour rather than empower and encourage (Matt. 7:15, NLT). His message is clear – bullying is not the way to achieve success: 'Whoever wants to be a leader among you must be your servant ...' (Matt. 20:26b, NLT). The apostle Paul spells out how we should conduct ourselves: 'Always be humble and gentle. Be patient with each other, making allowance for each other's faults because of your love' (Eph. 4:2, NLT). Requirements for leaders include: not being arrogant or quick-tempered; not being a heavy drinker, violent or dishonest with money (Titus 1:7, NLT). Rather they are to be hospitable, people who love what is good, who are self-controlled, upright, holy and disciplined (Titus 1:8).

What's required are 'servant leaders', who are very different from dictatorial leaders.

Servant leaders …
- Serve other people rather than themselves
- Find fulfilment in the accomplishments of others
- Are concerned with justice
- Do not 'break' people through their use of power
- Build a vision, not their own kingdom
- Do not discourage, but rather encourage
- Are not the centre of attention, but put others first
- Are fair and make sure all sides are heard

BREAKING FREE

When being bullied in an organisational context, it's not easy to walk away, for fear of repercussions. In addition, there may be the feeling that the target has invested time, money and energy into the church/organisation and has made good friends whom they don't want to fall out with or leave behind.

Even after someone has left, it takes time to heal. The effects of spiritual bullying are the same as for any type of bullying, but the person's experiences invariably raise serious questions about God, the church/organisation and their own faith. If you have suffered spiritual bullying do you tend to condemn yourself for not having been able to see what was happening earlier? Are you, at times, overcome by a sense of loss or feelings of injustice? Perhaps you have battled with guilt, anger, confusion, disappointment with God and lack of trust in those whom you assumed would prove trustworthy?

Helping yourself
Recovering from bullying, coming to terms with what has happened, and building trust and faith again can take a long time.

A few tips:
• **Break the 'don't talk' rule**
Bullies do not want you to talk to others. The spiritual bully will endeavour to evoke false guilt and spiritual consequences if you do. When you share your experiences with wise people it takes power away from a bully.

• **Try to find a 'safe person'**
It can be incredibly healing to have an *'anam cara'. Anam cara* is an Irish term meaning 'soul friend'. John O'Donohue explains it this way: 'The *anam cara* was a person to whom you could reveal the hidden intimacies of your life. This friendship was an act of recognition and belonging. When you had an *anam cara*, your friendship cut across all convention and category. You were joined in an ancient and eternal way with the friend of your soul'.[6]

• **Try to say 'No'**
Remember, it is God to whom you are accountable, not man. One of the most empowering things you can do is to say 'No'. Bullies expect those they control to be compliant. By saying 'No' you are disarming the bully.

• **Separate your view of God from the actions of the bully**
Spiritual bullying often carries the consequence of a distorted picture of God. The bully, if a spiritual leader, will not have been a healthy representation of godly character. Try to remind yourself that the bully's actions do not represent the nature of God.

REFLECTION
As well as hurting those of us who have been/are being bullied, it must hurt God profoundly that bullying happens by those who represent Him.

ACTION
When looking for godly leadership/people, remember that safe people are those who reflect the nature of God – who show the fruit of the Spirit in their lives: '... love, joy, peace, patience, kindness, goodness, faithfulness, gentleness and self-control' (Gal. 5:22–23).

PRAYER
I invite you to pray with me:
Dear God, I am so sorry that at times I blame You for the way others treat me. Help me to see You for who You really are and to separate You from the wrong actions of those who bully. Amen.

CHAPTER 6

TARGETS –
WHY THEY ARE PICKED

No one can make us feel inferior without our consent.

Eleanor Roosevelt[1]

VULNERABILITY

I remember asking myself, as do many people who are bullied, 'Why is this happening to *me*?' Well-meaning friends offered kind words of reassurance that it wasn't my problem. However, over time I came to realise that, as with other targets, there must be something in me that attracted domineering, controlling people. Perhaps you are also wondering what it is that draws bullies to you. Why not the girl/boy next to you or another work colleague? It's not because you are inferior in some way, as the bully would have you believe, but because either you are a threat to the bully or there is something in your life that allows the bully to latch on and take control.

Bullies will do all they can to crush your spirit, destroy your confidence and move you from being their target to becoming like putty in their hands – their mouldable victim. Even if you have been a *target* of bullying, you don't have to become a *victim*. Anyone can be a target of malicious actions, but becoming a victim means remaining passive, believing that you deserve to be bullied and making no attempt to understand why it's happening or to seek help. As a victim you are less likely to fight for your rights or to walk away from their controlling and manipulative vices; and you are therefore more likely to be bullied again.

TO WHAT DO BULLIES LATCH ON?

Bullies latch on to anything that stands out about a person or sets them apart in some way. Differences such as: ethnic/cultural background; religious beliefs; disability/deformity; sexual orientation; social class/accent; appearance/weight; intellect (high or low).

According to George Simon, author of *In Sheep's Clothing: Understanding and Dealing with Manipulative People*, bullies, or manipulators as he states, seek certain vulnerabilities in people:[2]

- **naivety** – victims find it too hard to accept the idea that some people are cunning, devious and ruthless, or are 'in denial' if they are being victimised
- **over-conscientiousness** – victims are too willing to give manipulators the benefit of the doubt and see their side of things in which they blame the victim
- **low self-confidence** – victims are self-doubting, lacking in confidence and assertiveness, likely to go on the defensive too easily
- **over-intellectualisation** – victims try too hard to believe the manipulator has some understandable reason to be hurtful

- **emotional dependency** – victims have a submissive or dependent personality. The more emotionally dependent the victim is, the more vulnerable he/she is to being exploited and manipulated.

In children, targets tend to be those who find it hard to make friends, are timid or insecure, have trouble sticking up for themselves or cry easily. Even children who have a tendency to lose control are ideal candidates because the bully gets a dramatic reaction. In adults, targets tend to be people who find it hard to defend themselves, have a low self-esteem, are easily deceived and controlled, or pose a threat to the bully in some way, such as being gifted.

CHARACTERISTICS ATTRACTIVE TO BULLIES

On the whole, the stronger you appear, the less interested bullies are, child or adult. The characteristics within targets which seem to attract bullies and enable them to sustain their attacks include:

1. Sensitivity

To bullies, sensitivity is highly seductive because the hurt caused by bullying is felt very deeply and is often easily seen on the target's face or in their body language. Being sensitive implies to the bully that the person is reactive, malleable and controllable.

When people are sensitive they take things to heart and are very aware of positive and negative atmospheres. Thoughtless or cruel words have a devastating effect and they find it difficult to shake off hurt feelings. Fears, doubts, thoughts all have the tendency to replay continuously; self-questioning and persecution easily take a hold and the person's head can be filled with the resounding echo of 'What's wrong with me?' The bully loves nothing better than to feel the power derived from seeing a sensitive person wounded by their 'masterful' actions.

2. Lack of self-confidence

People who are confident and secure in themselves are more able to ignore minor incidents and to communicate with others when people behave in potentially damaging ways. They also tend to be more comfortable in groups than those who lack confidence or are shy. Bullies are less likely to target someone who is secure and is surrounded by others.

In contrast, people who lack self-confidence are easier targets for bullies because they tend to look to others for direction. The bully, sensing the vulnerability of the target, may well take on the mantle of being a mentor – appearing strong and decisive and offering support. When the bully becomes controlling or abusive, the target feels trapped because of the supposed 'support' which the bully has previously offered.

3. Desire to please people

The kind of person who is bullied often wants to please others, maintain peace and establish harmony, which comes at the cost of playing into the hands of controlling people. Conflict may be avoided in order not to be hurt and to endeavour to be accepted by others. However, it becomes all too easy for the potential target to be drawn into a situation of being taken advantage of and, ultimately, bullied.

The target may also find it hard to trust their own judgment. Controlling people have tended to define what is right and wrong, causing the target to lose confidence in their own power of reasoning. They tend to feel that other people know better, which leads them to look to others for recognition, validation and decision making. This makes them highly susceptible to manipulation and criticism. When other people, as inevitably they do, tell the target that they are too sensitive or that they are reading into situations, it increases the target's doubt in their ability to judge events and allows confusion to set in.

Instilling confusion in the target is one of the bully's tactics, but when doubt and confusion already exist the bully's actions only worsen an already delicate way of perceiving life. This confusion and self-doubt result in the target finding it hard to accept fully that they are being bullied. Self-doubt is further increased when they attempt to tell someone that they are being bullied, and the person fails to believe them or to understand.

4. Easily intimidated
The most effective way for the bully to accomplish their need for a power difference is to evoke feelings of fear in the target. Those who get bullied are more easily intimidated than most by strong characters and their superior attitudes or 'put downs'. Consequently, bullies seek targets who are hesitant and socially anxious or, perhaps, quietly spoken. If the target can manage not to show that the harshness of the bully is getting to them, they are less likely to be pursued.

PAUSE FOR THOUGHT ...
Which character traits do you relate to? Remember not to condemn yourself for your traits; instead look at what it is within these that 'allows' bullies to 'latch on'. What could you do differently?

SET UP TO BE BULLIED

Some targets are from family backgrounds that are described as 'toxic'; in other words emotionally very unhealthy. The way the person is treated, the communication styles within the family, the poor expression of emotions and perhaps the parental control (carried out knowingly or unknowingly) damages the target and 'sets the person up' for bullying later on. Bullies can sense those who are 'ripe' for bullying. Dave Chapman calls such people 'followers'.

Qualities of followers:[3] 1. Good; 2. Idealistic; 3. Passive; 4. Self-critical; 5. Fearful; 6. Vulnerable.

1. Good – The bully wants followers who are co-operative, conscientious, giving and caring, people who are more likely to forgive the bully's aggression and continue serving their needs.

2. Idealistic – The best followers are naive, self-sacrificing and altruistic, with a strong belief in duty, obedience, loyalty and teamwork. A bully looks for people who are eager to please others in pursuit of a noble purpose (which, of course, is defined by the bully).

3. Passive – A bully wants followers who are polite, non-confrontational, afraid to debate with others openly, easily interrupted, quiet and non-expressive. They understand that introverts are more likely to become subservient to an aggressive leader.

4. Self-critical – People who are overly critical of themselves or lack self-respect are more likely to accept the premise that a bully has superior intellect and character. These types of followers tend to lack self-confidence, making them more willing to accept blame and become dependent on the leadership of the bully.

5. Fearful – People who display a great deal of fear are usually easier targets for intimidation and manipulation. As a result, a bully seeks followers who are tentative in manner and socially anxious, perhaps displaying nervous habits and speech patterns, such as using a timid tone of voice.

6. Vulnerable – Emotionally vulnerable people are more easily manipulated. Some of a bully's most loyal followers have difficult personal lives or long-term problems with their careers. Strong negative emotions – greed, anger, hate, envy, jealousy – also expose one to exploitation by a skilled bully.

PAUSE FOR THOUGHT ...
Is there anything in your family background which might have made you more vulnerable to bullying? Try to write your thoughts of what was done and by whom on the piece of paper I suggested you keep in the book (see page 16).

HEALING THE HURT
Being a target of bullying is soul-destroying at the time. In most cases it continues to erode the target's confidence or belief in themselves later in life too. If this is your experience, it's important to remember that what the bully has said and done does *not* define you. Words and actions may be cruel but they

cannot take away the very essence of who you are.

One of the more painful aspects of bullying and its effects is that you cannot change the bully's negative words and thoughts about you: many who have been bullied long to feel acceptable and liked after years of being put down. God Himself speaks the truth about you. Try to let these words heal some of the wounds in your heart.

> How precious are your thoughts about me, O God. They cannot be numbered! I can't even count them; they outnumber the grains of sand! And when I wake up, you are still with me!
>
> (Psa. 139:17–18, NLT)

REFLECTION

Are you aware that as a result of the pain of being bullied you may have taken on a 'victim mentality'? Do you believe that: you are helpless; your happiness is dependent on others; the grass is always greener somewhere else; someone needs to rescue you?

ACTION

Imagine all the accusatory words and wrongdoing of others as sticky plants which have been thrown at you and have stuck. You may have many. Say to yourself: 'I am not going to let these "sticky plants" remain on me'. See yourself pulling them off and throwing them away. They don't belong to you.

PRAYER

I invite you to pray with me:
Dear God, thank You that in Your eyes I am precious, loved and significant. I am not a helpless victim battered by the cruel actions of others. Amen.

CHAPTER 7

BULLIES – WHAT THEY ARE LIKE

Bullies are predators and choose their prey by homing in on vulnerability.

Tim Field[1]

TYPES OF BULLIES

Just as bullying takes different forms, so there are different types of bullies. Some are obnoxious and obvious in their bullying tactics; others are hard to identify because they operate 'under cover' – that is, on the surface they appear to be civil and co-operative, while they do everything in their power to undermine those they target. In summary, the bully can be:

- Aggressive: scream, threaten and blame – easily noticed
- Passive: subtle, divisive, undermining – hard to identify

A bully is like a sniffer-dog tracking fear, anxiety and submission: the scent of 'weakness' oozing from the target is highly appealing. For some bullies it doesn't matter what the 'weakness' is, as long as it gives rise to the bully witnessing powerlessness and the uncomfortable squirming of the target. For others, there is something *specific* in the target that triggers a need to take control, show aggression or re-enact events which have occurred in their own lives. A serial bully will go to incredible lengths to find something to 'home in on' in order to dominate and manipulate others.

One person, who years later admitted that he'd bullied as a child, summarised what was going on for him:

- There was a lot of pent-up frustration in me
- My home life wasn't exactly abusive, but it wasn't easy either
- My father had a temper and my older brother used to humiliate me and beat me up
- I usually picked on the kids that were loners or a bit 'weird'
- Most of them didn't seem to respect themselves, so it was easy to bully them
- It started with joking and winding people up and then progressed
- It felt 'cool' to bully, and others seemed to admire me for my 'toughness'
- I didn't really respect myself and I only felt good if I was 'top dog'
- I revelled in people's helplessness, perhaps because it made me feel more powerful
- I carried on bullying anyone who let me
- If someone stood up to me properly then I backed off. I didn't see them as weak any more

CHARACTERISTICS

There are common characteristics in people who bully, both in children and adults. Identifying these traits helps us all to become more aware of the people around us who have the potential to be bullies.

CHARACTERISTICS OF CHILD BULLIES

The child bully tends to question authority, break rules, be confrontational and persuasive, and push boundaries to their limits. Some child bullies are dominant and 'full of themselves', pushing other children around and believing that they are the best. Other bullies are actually insecure and put 'weaker' children down in order to make themselves feel better or to gain kudos and attract group members.

Dan Olweus identifies the characteristics of students who are most likely to be bullies:[2]

They have a strong need to dominate and subdue other students and to get their own way. Additionally, they:

- Are impulsive and easily angered
- Are often defiant and aggressive toward adults, including parents and teachers
- Show little empathy towards students who are victimised
- If they are boys, they are physically stronger than boys in general

CHARACTERISTICS OF ADULT BULLIES

Adult bullying is, perhaps, more complex than childhood bullying. In addition to the bully seeking someone they can dominate, mind games and hidden agendas are involved. It is said that adults who bully have personalities that are authoritarian, combined with a strong need to control.[3] Envy and resentment are also said to be motives for bullying,[4] but the driving force behind bullying is best summed up as 'a need for power'. The power which bullies crave, consciously or subconsciously, varies: dominance, presence, status, position, connection with influential people, as well as physical, emotional and spiritual superiority.

Just as bullying comes in all shapes and sizes, so do bullies. As we have already seen, there are aggressive and passive bullies. In addition, there are malicious and non-malicious bullies and bullies who have been victims themselves.

DOMINANT FEATURES

Whilst there may be different types of bullies, most exhibit some common features. Do these seem familiar to you?

1. Jekyll and Hyde nature;
2. Need to be in charge;
3. Self-focused.

1. Jekyll and Hyde nature

The double-sided nature of most bullies, charming and vindictive, makes it far harder to see bullying for what it is. Perhaps you have experienced the 'Jekyll and Hyde' nature of the bully: sucked in by the person's charm only to later experience their cruelty and control.

If bullies were consistently malicious it would make spotting and walking away from them much easier. Since there is 'double-sidedness' to the bully, some people (who are not targets) may not have seen the 'unpleasant' side of the bully, which makes it even more difficult for the target to be believed when speaking up about what has happened. 'But he's such a nice man,' the other person exclaims, 'I can't imagine him treating anyone badly.' The 'Jekyll and Hyde' nature shows itself when what was said in one situation is vehemently denied in another. The target is the one made to appear to be acting divisively or deceptively; and those who only know the 'nice' side of the bully may well believe that the bully is right.

One person explains the chain of events which resulted in her realising that she was being bullied by a 'Jekyll and Hyde' person. Her director, a woman, had a charisma about her which caused people to want to be around her.

- She was dynamic – powerful and successful – and at first took an extra interest in me. She was supportive, helpful and kind.
- She created an illusion of being the only reliable person and caused me to doubt the stability and reliability of other people.
- If there was disunity in the organisation, somehow she always seemed to come out as the one who rescued the situation – a hero.
- She was charming until I 'crossed her', picked up on inconsistencies or didn't bend over backwards to please her.
- When I stopped putting her on a pedestal, *everything* changed.
- It was inferred that I was untrustworthy. I was ostracised and my name was blackened.
- Any attempts I made to put the situation right resulted in accusations of me being 'paranoid'.
- She controlled me and spoke negatively about me to others.
- For me, the only way out was to leave. Even so, there was a long-lasting effect as my name was tarnished.
- She was influential in the line of work I was in, and several years later I was still being judged and misrepresented by people with whom she had been in contact.

PAUSE FOR THOUGHT ...

Do these characteristics remind you of anyone in your life? Have you talked to anyone about your experiences? I would encourage you not to carry the weight of being bullied alone.

2. Need to be in charge

The bully has a driving need to set the agenda, exercise authority and take control. Anyone who disagrees or is perceived by the bully as a potential threat is quickly undermined and discredited. Personal decisions are not allowed to be made by the target; if they are, they are quickly quashed. Another tactic used is divisiveness; if two people are questioning the actions of the bully then there is often an attempt by the bully to cause the two people to attack or doubt each other.

Some bullies attempt very obviously to control not just what a person does but what they think and believe. Guilt and fear are common tools used to succeed in getting their own way. If a bully is not in control it disturbs them because it means loss of power and no longer being 'top dog'. For them, being dominant also keeps personal insecurities hidden.

3. Self-focused

The type of person who bullies is someone who can be described as 'I' focused. The world revolves around them and their aspirations, often at the expense of the needs of others. They may portray themselves as kind and concerned, but in truth their actions are more often in contrast. There is a clear discrepancy between how they like other people to perceive them and how they actually come across. Very often they are blatantly unaware of the difference.

Bullies do not accept responsibility for their own actions or feelings – it's always the other person's fault. In this way they cast blame for how they feel – '*You* make me so cross' – and shame others – 'You're useless'.

Bullies in leadership positions demonstrate what they think are leadership skills but, in fact, these 'skills' tend to be based around anger, impulsiveness and lack of transparency. The target is left feeling fearful and obligated. This is very different from healthy leadership, which shows itself through integrity, humility, maturity and decisiveness, and which encourages trust and respect.

PAUSE FOR THOUGHT ...

Whilst bullying is very wrong, the bully can still have positive aspects to them, even if hard to see at the time. What words would you use to describe the person a) when bullying you and b) when not acting as a bully?

In addition to the dominant features just mentioned, Dave Chapman highlights visible and hidden traits of bullies.[5]

Visible traits:
- Controls others
- Very ambitious
- Overly confident
- Strong-willed
- Argumentative
- Judgmental
- Highly critical

Hidden traits:
- Charming
- Obsessed with image
- Distorts truth and reality
- Evasive
- Plays the victim
- Self-righteous and hypocritical

- Two-faced
- Rumour-monger
- Passive-aggressive
- Pretends to care

VISIBLE TRAITS

Controls others: micromanages; dominates conversations; prevents communication; is territorial; uses the target's emotions; affection and support come at a price; endeavours to live the target's life for the person.

Very ambitious: can seem possessed by the desire to achieve power and success; constantly seeks to add to their power base; tries to gain power over peers; entices the target with false promises.

Overly confident: likely to possess a high level of self-confidence and self-satisfaction, which contribute to their overbearing nature; arrogance, intellectual narcissism, a self-glorifying attitude and praising of self-accomplishments.

Strong-willed: constantly pressurises others to change their thinking and yield to the bully's objectives and demands; insists that only their suggestions are reasonable; when the bully thinks their ideas are being attacked, they attack the target personally.

Argumentative: feels compelled to force their opinions on others; challenges and contradicts other people's ideas; misrepresents the other person's viewpoint; implies the target is misleading others; quotes conversations out of context etc.

Judgmental: tends to pass judgment on other people's actions and intentions; diligently repeats someone else's criticism of the target regardless of its validity; suggests that a single comment reflects everyone's viewpoint.

Highly critical: keeps others on the defensive through constant criticism; grinds people into submission, attacking the person's integrity and reliability.

HIDDEN TRAITS

Charming: charms others to gain their trust; their charismatic personality provides an excellent disguise, resulting in most people readily accepting the fiction of their good intentions rather than the reality of their self-serving nature.

Obsessed with image: tends to be obsessed with how things appear to others; their obsession causes them to overreact to actions or comments that they believe are a threat to their carefully crafted image.

Distorts truth and reality: puts a positive spin on their own behaviour and intentions, whilst implying the worst about the behaviours and intentions of the target – making them appear reasonable and constructive, while the target appears unreasonable and destructive.

Evasive: never gives a straight answer about their bullying behaviour, if challenged; denies their self-serving intentions and acts confused by complaints about their mistreatment of others; questions the motives of the complainer; undermines the target behind their back.

Plays the victim: acts like a victim in order to manipulate others into submitting to their own desires; repeatedly mentions any actions of the target which have caused hurt or difficulty, particularly when they want to manipulate the target into going along with their plans.

Self-righteous and hypocritical: tends to be self-righteous and hypocritical, implying that they are a good person, but others are ill-intentioned and devious; tells stories that demonstrate their own goodness and highlight the questionable motives of others.

Two-faced: positive and supportive in public, but negative and overly critical in private; others sing praises of their virtue, vision, good humour and leadership, while the target is suffering from the bully's frequent attempts to intimidate and belittle.

Rumour-monger: commonly undermines the target behind their back to reduce their power; spreads damaging rumours when they want to weaken the target permanently; criticises character of target; repeats unwarranted negative comments about the target.

Passive-aggressive: may be aggressive towards the target by things they *don't* do; by not doing something that would normally occur, the bully can insult and weaken the target; their intention is to make others feel guilty.

Pretends to care: conceals their destructive behaviours under an exterior of charm and friendliness. Some of the ways the bully attacks under the guise of pretending to care are:

- Belittling the target in a 'friendly' manner
- Giving overly harsh criticism, disguised as 'friendly advice'
- Offering to give helpful feedback, then making a malicious statement

TAKING A STAND

Hopefully, as we all become more aware of the nature of the bully, we can take a stand against bullying and pull back from being sucked into the destructive spirals which occur. Without a victim, there is no bullying. Whilst we can't stop people dominating, controlling and carrying out emotionally disruptive interactions, we can all recognise the warning signs and look at how best to respond.

REFLECTION

It's easy to see the bully as 'the enemy' and to operate from a continuously defensive or fear-driven response. Instead, try to view the bully as an 'ordinary' person who needs help to change. The bully has less power than our minds would have us believe.

ACTION

Recall a time when you were bullied and the responses and wording you may have used to deal with the situation. Now try to write a new script, this time from a position of viewing the bully as having less power and you having a voice to speak up.

PRAYER

I invite you to pray with me:

Dear God, I cannot fight this battle. I hand it over to You. I give over to You those who have bullied me in the past and those who continue to bully me now. The battle belongs to You. I ask You to bring about change and to help me to be less defensive and fearful. Amen.

CHAPTER 8

EFFECTS - IMPACT ON THE MIND AND BODY

Feelings are much like waves, we can't stop them from coming but we can choose which one to surf.

Jonatan Mårtensson[1]

EMOTIONAL ROLLERCOASTER

Bullying impacts the mind and emotions more powerfully than perhaps we realise. Whilst bullies may feel empowered and exhilarated by their actions, targets are thrown into a turbulent emotional world.

Amidst the whirl of scathing remarks, backstabbing, manipulation and control, the target may feel confused, shocked, stressed, unsafe, hopeless, sad, guilty, lonely, anxious, ashamed, angry, worthless, desperate and overcome by grief. The rollercoaster of emotions sets up the target for internal chaos and results in them feeling permanently 'on guard'.

THOUGHTS BEHIND FEELINGS

The intense emotions (which may at times be numbed) do not occur in isolation but are fed by thoughts: beliefs that the target has acquired over the years and which are emphasised through the bullying. If the thoughts can be challenged, then the feelings, though still there, will most likely be less intense. It is a well-known fact that behind negative feelings lie negative thoughts.

Thought	Feeling
I can't ever get anything right	Failure
I'm not as acceptable as other people	Inferiority
There's something wrong with me	Shame
I'm always rejected	Worthlessness
People don't like me or want to include me	Rejection
It's going to happen again	Anxiety
I will get hurt, rejected, used	Fear
I can't get out of this	Hopelessness

When the destructive words spoken by a bully are constantly repeated or are similar to those said to the target in other abusive situations, they become reinforced. The words: 'You don't belong in our group' get translated into 'I'm not wanted by anyone'. The feeling of not being wanted eats into the person and soon their whole demeanour has an air of 'leave me alone' about it. The trouble is, people then do. This heightens the sense of not being included.

CHALLENGING THE LIES

It's natural that the target's thinking will be dominated by the words and behaviour of the bully but, if the pattern is to be broken, it is important that the thoughts which feed negative emotions are challenged. The following chart is a fictional account of someone who is being bullied at work and who was also bullied at school. It is a classic example of how past experiences of bullying feed the person's feelings about their present experience, resulting in ingrained negative beliefs.

School experiences	Work experiences	Beliefs	Correction
The school bully:	*The manager:*	*The target thinks:*	*The targets needs to say:*
Sent the target to 'Coventry'	Ignores the target and talks to other people	'There's something unacceptable about me'	'The manager has the problem; I'm not unacceptable'
Put the target down in front of friends	Undermines the target in front of colleagues	'I'm obviously not good enough'	'This makes the manager feel better – it's not about me'
Lied about the target to friends and teachers	Misrepresents and misinterprets the target	'People will never see the real me'	'People who matter will see me for who I am'
Told the target they were useless	Devalues what the target does	'I can never get anything right'	'I have rights and abilities, like anyone else'

LONG-TERM CONSEQUENCES

The bullying itself may be relatively short-lived but the physical and mental effects can last for years. They can erode a person's trust in people, as well as weaken the person's ability to cope.

PAUSE FOR THOUGHT ...

Have you noticed any particular changes, physically or emotionally, since being bullied? It's important to discover ways to look after and nurture yourself so that your body does not become too stressed.

Research indicates that: 'Being a victim of bullying in childhood is associated with poorer mental health outcomes, such as depression and anxiety, poorer functioning in social and occupational roles and greater likelihood of repeatedly thinking about suicide in adulthood.'[2] In addition, targets of bullying are more prone to panic attacks and lowered resistance to infection due to high stress levels.

Some people who are bullied, particularly if their experiences are severe or long-lasting, end up traumatised, resulting in disturbing thoughts, images and flashbacks. They may find themselves reliving past events, as though still happening in the present. When in that situation, they have a heightened sense of danger, anticipating the worst, and may feel anxious and insecure or have angry outbursts at inappropriate moments. The energy required to live each day with the unresolved trauma is hugely draining, both physically and emotionally, and can result in being emotionally detached and feeling hopeless.

Signs to look out for:
1. Stress and fatigue
2. Depression
3. Distorted view of self and life
4. Destructive coping strategies
5. Post-Traumatic Stress Disorder (PTSD)

1. Stress and fatigue
The word 'stress' is derived from the Latin word *stringere* meaning 'to draw tight'. It was used during the seventeenth century in reference to affliction and hardship. The effects of bullying cause the target to feel that everything is being 'drawn tight' and their whole system is on overload.

To understand stress requires differentiating between stress and pressure. We experience *pressure* most days of our lives and it's actually needed to motivate us and help us to be productive. However, if we experience too much pressure with little chance of recovery then we encounter *stress* – the feeling that things are 'getting on top' of us and we are overloaded.

Stress affects a person's perceptions and judgments, making it more difficult to consider alternatives in life and make constructive choices. The effects of stress can include:

Physical and behavioural effects: tiredness, headaches, dizziness, difficulty sleeping, constipation/diarrhoea, change in eating patterns, cramps/muscle spasms, chest/back pains, restlessness, breathlessness, skin irritations, high blood pressure, sweating, nervous habits, sexual difficulties, and dependency on mood-altering substances to cope.

Emotional and relational effects: anxiety and panic attacks, anger, depression, guilt, emotional numbness, tearfulness, hypervigilance, hypersensitivity, difficulty concentrating, indecisiveness, forgetfulness, feeling powerless to change things, low self-worth, sense of life being unfair, loss of sense of humour, feeling isolated/abandoned, being critical of, or finding it hard to get on with, others.

The person with a trauma history or several encounters of bullying is highly susceptible to stress. Tim Field points out that there are at least four factors which determine the degree to which one will feel stressed, all of which fit bullying:[3]

- *control:* a person feels stressed to the extent to which they perceive they are not in control of the stressor; at work, employees have no control over their management
- *predictability:* a person feels stressed to the extent to which they are unable to predict the behaviour or occurrence of the stressor (bullies are notoriously unpredictable in their behaviour)
- *expectation:* a person feels stressed to the extent to which they perceive their circumstances are not improving and will not improve
- *support:* a person feels stressed to the extent to which they lack support systems, including work colleagues, management, personnel, union, partner, family, friends, colleagues, persons in authority, official bodies, professionals, and the law

PAUSE FOR THOUGHT ...
What helps you, as an individual, to reduce stress and lessen its effects?
- Taking mini-breaks?
- Having a soak in the bath?

- Listening to music?
- Taking a walk in a peaceful place?

What additional thing are you going to commit to doing to relieve stress?

2. Depression

Depression affects both children and adults. Research shows that 'compared to their peers, kids who are bullied are five times more likely to be depressed'.[4] Research also reveals that someone who is bullied typically suffers from depression later in life. Researchers from the University of Florida carried out a study on 210 college students and discovered a link between what psychologists call relational victimisation in adolescence and depression and anxiety in early adulthood.[5]

People who are depressed often struggle to think clearly or to recognise their own symptoms.

Symptoms of depression include:
- Sadness and tearfulness
- Worry and anxiety
- Feelings of worthlessness and emptiness
- A sense of helplessness and powerlessness
- Loss of interest or pleasure in normal activities
- Pessimism and negativity
- Low energy or drive (including sexual)
- Poor communication and difficulty relating to others
- Withdrawal or isolation from people and social activities
- Acute sensitivity to failure and feeling guilty
- Poor concentration and daydreaming

- Difficulty in sleeping or finding it hard to get up
- Changes in appetite and eating patterns
- Physical symptoms: aches and pains, upset stomach etc
- Difficulty making decisions
- Self-destructive thoughts

It is known that there is a link between this feeling of helplessness and depression. This feeling is lessened or counteracted by the person having a sense of control over their circumstances. For this reason it is important that the target is encouraged to work on what they *can* change, rather than focus on what they are unable to change at the moment.

3. Distorted view of self and life
Targets may find it hard to believe in themselves. This is because they have integrated into their belief system the negative viewpoint of the bully and other people. Perhaps you know how that feels and now you are unsure what to think about yourself, life or other people.

The uncertainties and insecurities can also affect the target's ability to push through difficult circumstances, leaving them in a position of perceived powerlessness and feeling trapped. The longer the bullying continues and the more bullies the target encounters, the greater the impact on the person's sense of confidence, value, worth and identity. The bullying may have come to an end some time ago but the consequences carry on, leaving the target in an almost continuous state of self-doubt, fear and anxiety.

PAUSE FOR THOUGHT ...

We often struggle to see the positive in our lives. Can you think of a well-balanced, kind person you know who could help you to look at the positives in you?

4. Destructive coping strategies

Amidst the trauma of bullying the target has to find some way to cope. They may not have had healthy ways of coping modelled to them and they find themselves using destructive coping strategies, such as:

- Withdrawal and isolation
- Abuse of alcohol
- Misuse of prescription drugs/use of illicit drugs
- Eating disorders
- Self-harm

Self-destructive behaviour is any kind of action carried out by the person towards themselves that is harmful. It is a broad term that includes self-injury, such as cutting and burning oneself and taking overdoses. It can also involve abusive relationships and addictions. The largest survey of its kind to date was carried out by the eating disorder charity, 'Beat'. The survey involved 600 young people with eating disorders. Of those surveyed, 91% had experienced bullying and 46% felt it contributed to their eating disorder. Nearly half were bullied over a period of 2–5 years and 11% for 6 years or more.[6] (For further information on eating disorders, see my book *Beyond Chaotic Eating*).

The emotional pain encountered in bullying and the negative impact can be so intolerable that targets not only suffer from addictive and self-harming behaviour but have thoughts of suicide (suicidal ideation) or actually commit suicide (bullycide). Tragically, 'suicide is a permanent solution to a temporary situation'.[7] Had those who had taken their lives been heard, understood and helped their stories might have been different. The stark reality is that some people can't find the courage or the help to end their nightmare; and sadly the weight they carry in terms of the effects of bullying is too great. They remove themselves in an attempt to remove the pain.

If you feel suicidal ...

Call The Samaritans on 08457 90 90 90

If living outside the UK, visit www.befrienders.org to find the helpline for your country.

It is said that victims of bullying are more likely to have attempted suicide than their non-bullied peers.[8] Tim Field states: 'Each year in the UK over 5,000 people take their life. Suicide statistics show that in the UK at least 16 children kill themselves each year because they are being bullied at school ... The number of adults who commit suicide because of bullying, harassment and violence is unknown, but my guess is that bullying is a factor in a significant number of these 5,000 suicides.'[9]

5. Post-Traumatic Stress Disorder (PTSD)

Psychological trauma, particularly where there is loss of control and disempowerment, may result in an acute stress reaction. For some people this leads to Post-Traumatic Stress Disorder (PTSD).

PTSD is characterised by four primary symptoms:[10]

Intrusion: Recurrent recollections of the event

- Dreams, intrusive memories, and exaggerated emotional and physical reactions to events that remind person of trauma

Numbing: Emotional distancing from surrounding people and events
- Depression, loss of interest in activities, reduced ability to feel emotions (particularly emotions of intimacy, tenderness, or sexuality), irritability, hopelessness

Avoidance: Fear and avoidance behaviour
- Fear and avoidance of people, places, thoughts, or activities associated with the trauma, development of anxiety disorders (GAD [generalised anxiety disorder], panic, specific and social phobias)

Arousal: Agitated state of constant wakefulness and alertness
- Hypervigilance, sleep disturbances, difficulty concentrating

Essentially PTSD results from an overwhelming onslaught on the mind and emotions. It was first associated with veterans of war who experienced 'shell shock'. Later it was noted that people who encountered other traumas exhibited similar symptoms. However, where there is repeated trauma it was noted that additional symptoms, such as changes in their self-concept and the way they adapt to stressful events, were evident. For this reason Dr Judith Herman of Harvard University suggests that a new diagnosis, Complex PTSD, is needed to describe the symptoms of long-term trauma.[11] My thoughts are that ongoing bullying would fit this description.

Not everyone who experiences trauma will develop PTSD or Complex PTSD. Why some do and some don't is not fully known, although it is suggested that personality type, a family history of depression/anxiety and a stressful lifestyle are all factors.

The long-term consequences of bullying can be devastating. Where there has been extensive bullying it can take many years for a person to recover. Like many traumas, recovery and healing doesn't 'just happen' but occurs with specific input, some of which we will explore in more detail in later chapters of the book.

REFLECTION
When a stone is thrown into a pond there are ripples which follow, even after the stone has sunk. In the same way the effects of bullying can continue – even after the bullying has ended.

ACTION
If you are able, write down the various ripples from your encounters with bullying (emotional wounds and stress reactions etc). For which of these do you consider you still need help? Is there any action you can take to further the healing process?

PRAYER
I invite you to pray with me:
Jesus, You were humiliated, ridiculed and bullied. You understand my many wounds which, at times, cause so much pain. I ask You to show me Your presence during the times when I was being bullied and to bring Your healing in a way that no one else can. Amen.

CHAPTER 9

BULLYING CYCLE - WHY PATTERNS ARE REPEATED

Courage is fire, and bullying is smoke.

Benjamin Disraeli[1]

FURTHER WOUNDS

For some people bullying is a one-off occurrence – perhaps taking place at school or work for a period of weeks or months. However, for a great many bullying occurs in more than one context and over a number of years. The more I have thought about bullying with its associated patterns, the more I have seen it in terms of a cycle. What I have devised are four stages which I consider most applicable to the Bullying Cycle. At each stage there are usually further wounds. If the cycle is not broken at one of the stages, it is likely to repeat itself or create another unhealthy one, leading to further abusive situations in the person's life.

THE BULLYING CYCLE

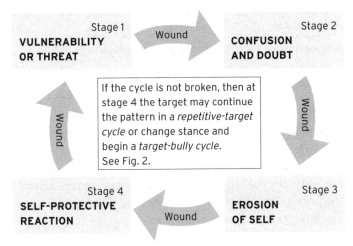

Fig. 1

THE BULLYING CYCLE EXPLAINED

STAGE 1: VULNERABILITY OR THREAT

The bullying cycle begins with an entry point:

a) an area of vulnerability within the target of which the bully takes advantage

b) a threat the target poses to the bully. The bully becomes hooked into that particular individual and the cycle begins.

Entry point: *vulnerability*	Entry point: *threat*
Lack of confidence	Conscientious/gifted
Shyness/insecurity	High moral standards
Emotional vulnerability	Opposing opinions to the bully
Something which causes the target to stand out from the crowd	Ability to see flaws in the bully

STAGE 2: CONFUSION AND DOUBT

Once hooked in, the bully begins the barrage of attacks. The danger here is that the attacks are camouflaged in such a way that it's difficult to define as bullying; and the target is left in a place of uncertainty. 'Is it bullying, or isn't it?' 'Is it just my interpretation?' In the uncertainty, the target may justify the bullying:

- 'The other person doesn't mean it'
- 'I must have done something wrong'
- 'I'm a weak person'
- 'I'm not as likeable as other people'
- 'If I hadn't done this/said that then it would have been OK'

As the bullying continues the stunned target tries to make sense of what is happening but often finds themselves going round and round in circles. At this stage, the target can feel somewhat chaotic. The confusion and self-doubt place the target in an even more vulnerable position.

STAGE 3: EROSION OF SELF

As the bullying continues, the damage sets in. The undermining, intimidation, manipulation, unkindness and underhandedness cut into the target and there is an erosion of self. One person, who'd been bullied at school, church and work, said of the effect of bullying: 'It makes me feel like I'm shrinking and confirms the negative beliefs I have about myself.' Another drew a picture of how she felt. The image was of a downcast woman who had chunks carved out of her body. She said it felt as if the bullying had eaten away at her, and had stolen her health and wellbeing.

The destruction takes various forms: the person's confidence is shredded, hope is diminished and life is sucked out. Sometimes, at this stage, the target will do what they can to try to rectify the situation. They may carry out people-pleasing behaviour in an attempt to appease the bully and win favour. Alternatively they may try to challenge the actions of the bully, but fail to realise that dealing with a bully is different from dealing with the average person. Either way the attempts fail.

STAGE 4: SELF-PROTECTIVE REACTION

As wounds accumulate there will be a self-protective reaction within the target. Depending on the nature of the target and other factors, the reaction will be either passive or aggressive (see Fig. 2). A passive response comes from the person who feels powerless and needs to be rescued. Typically they re-enter the bullying cycle and end up being bullied, again and again. They may go on to develop a victim mentality, always feeling that they're the one who is picked on and allowing bullies to get their way.

An aggressive response is more likely to stem from the person who, in their anger, has the desire to punish others. They may leave the original bullying cycle and start another one in which they intimidate others (target-bully cycle). Whether the person remains a victim or becomes a bully as a part of a new cycle, they negate healing.

SELF-PROTECTIVE REACTIONS

PASSIVE: REPETITIVE-TARGET CYCLE

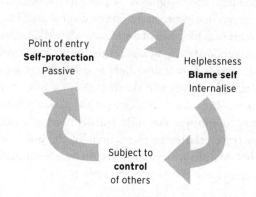

Point of entry
Self-protection
Passive

Helplessness
Blame self
Internalise

Subject to
control
of others

AGGRESSIVE: TARGET-BULLY CYCLE

Point of entry
Self-protection
Aggressive

Helplessness
Blame others
Externalise

Need to
control
others

Fig. 2

REPETITIVE-TARGET CYCLE

The person who remains unable to fight back or walk away from bullying is in a constant state of vulnerability and at risk of being bullied. Their style of self-protection sets them up for living in a state of helplessness. They internalise the pain and quickly blame themselves, holding on to the belief that there is essentially something wrong with them. This makes them subject to the control of others; and hence they are repeatedly intimidated and manipulated.

A badly treated wounded animal will shy away from people, but if pushed too far may bite. In the same way, the person caught on the repetitive-target cycle in the main will be passive, but may at times 'bite back'. These attempts usually backfire and wound the target even more.

TARGET-BULLY CYCLE

The target whose nature is more proactive or aggressive may break away from the original bullying cycle to victimise others. In this case, moving away from being a target is not a sign of healing because the target-bully is trying to gain lost power in order to feel better. The target-bully becomes reactive, blaming others rather than themselves; externalising rather than internalising their pain, and punishing others for what they've gone through. They may no longer be subject to the control of others, but they have an overriding need to control in order to survive. Some people simultaneously remain a target in one setting and act as a bully in another, in order to compensate.

PAUSE FOR THOUGHT ...
A sense of power is gained through breaking the bullying cycle. Looking back, at each stage of the cycle, explore what you could have done differently.

DESTRUCTIVE SPIRALS
At each point of the bullying cycle there is the potential for destructive spirals to develop: a chain reaction which is set up in the person as a result of the trauma, such as:

a) Grief
Grief occurs in the context of loss: the target has been robbed of joy, security, safety and healthy interaction with others. With prolonged bullying, the danger is that not only does the target experience loss at the time the destructive actions are being carried out, but also they begin to perceive the world through the mindset of 'things having been taken away'. The person can end up living with a perpetual sense of loss and the expectation that happiness won't last.

Whilst it's vital that the target gets in touch with their loss, it's also important that they don't become swamped by it. Help may be needed to break the spiral through encouraging the person to see that what has been lost is only *one* part of their life, not the *whole* of their life.

b) Anger
Anger is a normal and healthy reaction to being hurt and it's important that it's expressed in a constructive way. The person needs to be able to state what they are angry about, but not take their anger out on others or on themselves. However, some

people get caught in an anger spiral: rather than their anger being justified and the expression of it therapeutic, the anger consumes the person and leads to bitterness. When someone is caught in this spiral, the world is viewed as punitive (believing that others want to punish them) and they expect the worst on every occasion. There is a deep sense that life or situations are unfair and that other people are better off than they are. The person tends to be defensive and to feel permanently hard done by. Their behaviour and interactions with others can come across as accusatory and untrusting, doing further damage to everyday relationships.

c) Fear

Being wounded by another human being (especially when the wounding is ongoing) results in fear, lack of trust and expectation of further hurt. The target may well find a spiral of fear developing whereby they not only fear the bully but people in general. They may project onto healthy relationships the hurt encountered through bullying and end up being reactive towards others. A raised voice or the thought of being misunderstood, even by someone other than the bully, can be sufficient for some targets to become fearful and suffer from anxiety.

d) Unhealthy relating

Any kind of unkindness from other individuals not only causes deep wounds, but inner needs: the need for inclusion, affirmation and love. When these needs fail to be met in straightforward ways, the person can find themselves in a spiral of unhealthy relating: using patterns of avoidance, bargaining and manipulation. This is both damaging to the target and those with whom they interact. It is in the chaos of 'messy' relating that the target may be setting themselves up for further bullying – with the same bully or with someone else.

In taking a brief look at the Bullying Cycle, we have seen how easy it is for a target to go on being victimised or to take out their anger and need for power on someone else. The good news is that the cycle *can* be broken and new patterns established, helping to minimise the risk of further bullying in the future. Fighting back from bullying requires courage to see yourself as you really are – precious and worthy. Harvey Forbes Fierstein, an American actor and playwright, once said: 'Never be bullied into silence. Never allow yourself to be made a victim. Accept no one's definition of your life, but define yourself'.[2]

REFLECTION

In reading about the Bullying Cycle, which parts spoke to you the most?

ACTION

If you were helping someone who was stuck at a particular point on the cycle, what advice would you give them? Can you choose to apply the same advice to yourself?

PRAYER

I invite you to pray with me:
Dear God, I don't want to keep going round on this cycle. Please help me to recognise what is causing me to stay on the cycle. Amen.

CHAPTER 10

BREAKING THE CYCLE

The bullying stopped when I claimed myself and proved that I wasn't afraid.

Randy Harrison[1]

SAYING IT AS IT IS

People find all sorts of ways to describe their bullying experiences, other than using the word 'bullying'. Instead of saying 'I'm being bullied' (or if it's in the past, 'I was bullied'), the target may say:

- 'Things aren't quite right'
- 'I don't think I'm treated the same as other people, but it might just be me'
- 'Everyone would say it's a bit of a harsh environment'
- 'I'm not happy, but I'm probably oversensitive'
- 'It's tough, but it probably is in most places'
- 'So and so seems a bit controlling'
- 'It's probably my fault that things aren't working out'
  There is no better word for the wrong action of one individual

towards another than *bullying*. However, using the word, when being bullied yourself, isn't necessarily easy. Perhaps, reading this book has made you realise that you've never actually owned the fact that your experiences equate to bullying. Instead you've carried a burden without a name. Or maybe you have a friend (or are helping someone) who has also carried a burden without a name: could you help them to see that their experiences equate to bullying?

ADMITTING THE IMPACT

As well as being able to own the fact that you were bullied, it's helpful to face the truth about the way you've been treated. If you were bullied, what words would you use to describe the actions of the bully? Putting names to your experience makes it more real. Although, understandably, you may want to avoid reality, it's only through coming face-to-face with it that you can heal. Tick the words that apply.

I encountered …
☐ Intimidation
☐ Manipulation
☐ Control
☐ Misuse of power/abuse of authority
☐ Emotional blackmail
☐ Emotional/physical abuse
☐ Deceit/distorted truth/outright lies
☐ Unkindness/cruelty
☐ Demands and threats
☐ Being 'taken over'/consumed
☐ Being misjudged/misrepresented
☐ Being ignored, left out, ostracised

FEELING THE FEELINGS

Bullying brings with it a host of emotions. Thinking about your experience of bullying, which words jump out at you?

Alienated	Stubborn	Affectionate	Indifferent
Grumpy	Abused	Unhappy	At ease
Vulnerable	Degraded	Horrified	Inadequate
Discounted	Anxious	Annoyed	Appealing
Appreciated	Ashamed	Disgusted	Guilty
Bored	Bad	Moody	Bitter
Fearful	Bewildered	Brave	Concerned
Contented	Confused	Compelled	Kind
Nervous	Relieved	Disappointed	Consoled
Controlled	Abandoned	Happy	Dejected
Daring	Dreadful	Angry	Detested
Delighted	Determined	Fearless	Dismayed
Driven	Negative	Rebellious	Amused
Dependent	Overcommitted	Self-conscious	Loved
Dissatisfied	Peaceful	Embarrassed	Mixed up
Envious	Edgy	Exhausted	Worthless
Good	Excited	Provoked	Apprehensive
Independent	Fed up	Frustrated	Tense
Uncomfortable	Lonely	Worried	Stupid
Hopeless	Miserable	Harassed	Superior
Wanted	Hated	Threatened	Trapped
Hopeful	Troubled	Torn	Hurt
Useless	Impatient	Indecisive	Rejected
Courageous	Childish	Indignant	Inhibited
Resentful	Joyful	Helpless	Cynical
Unimportant	Liked	Humiliated	Scared
Unwanted	Respected	Unpopular	Unloved
Reluctant	Optimistic	Secure	Shy
Paranoid	Sympathetic	Sad	Understood
Reflective	Patient	Puzzled	Valuable
Proud	Relaxed	Timid	Vengeful

For those who have been victimised it may be helpful to ask the following questions:

- What emotions did I feel whilst being bullied?
- What emotions do I feel now?
- How do I respond to painful emotions?
- Do I tend to express positive emotions and conceal negative ones?
- How can I express these without hurting others or myself?
- Were the actions of the bully right?
- Who was responsible – me or the bully?
- Am I still justifying the bully's behaviour?
- At what point could I have broken the cycle?
- What could I have done differently?
- What do I need to change to prevent bullying happening again?

PAUSE FOR THOUGHT ...

Some people find that images and pictures help them to understand how they feel. Have you thought of keeping a journal as a beneficial way to process the impact of the bullying? Remember to try to write something positive about your day too!

FACING BLOCKAGES

Changing patterns and reactions is not easy. No doubt there will be conflicting feelings: wanting to be free from bullying but, at the same time, feeling insecure about stepping outside the comfort of known reactions. When someone changes the way they relate, other people often change their response – and not always for the better. If, for instance, someone who has always been passive learns to be more assertive, there may be some people (not just the bully) who preferred the person in a more submissive state and whose reactions make life uncomfortable. The thought of friction/conflict is sometimes enough to keep the target in old patterns. Some targets choose to remain victims because they don't know how to live without a victim mentality.

Both the bully and the target may find it hard to alter instinctive reactions because the behaviour is not only ingrained but it also has a pay-off. A pay-off simply means that the current way of behaving does something 'helpful' for the person. Facing reality involves considering the pay-offs in staying on the bullying cycle. For the bully, the pay-offs are quite clear: feeling in control; gaining status; compensating for inadequacies; and, in some cases, impressing others.

There are a number of pay-offs for the target too, including:

- **Avoiding conflict** The target is someone who finds it hard to fight back and likes to keep the peace. To stay on the bullying cycle, although extremely unpleasant, is a way of avoiding conflict; to break the cycle has the potential for confrontation and criticism.

- **Maintaining vulnerability** On the whole, people don't go out of their way to be vulnerable in order to be comforted. However, some people, having experienced vulnerability, hold onto it in order to feel cared for by others.

- **Masking other abusive situations** Sometimes staying on the bullying cycle covers up other abusive situations from the past, since the focus is centred on the current bullying. For those targets who have been bullied by a number of different people over the years, endeavouring to break the cycle feels too difficult. It seems easier simply to keep things as they are, even if the target is desperately unhappy.

RESTORING WORTH

The greater impact of bullying is most often on the target's self-esteem and self-confidence. Bullies feast off lack of confidence: the more the target can strengthen this area, the greater their ability to put in place healthy barriers and move off the cycle. Bullying undermines, so combating it and its effects is going to involve helping the target to develop an accurate picture of what they are like and the abilities they have.

Restoring self-confidence and self-worth is required to help protect against bullying, to withstand it when it does happen, and to heal from it after it has occurred. Positive input counterbalances negative input by the bully and facilitates the process of the target being able to feel and act in a less down-trodden manner.

Bullying ...	Self-confidence ...
Questions your abilities	Affirms your abilities
Focuses on your weaknesses	Focuses on your strengths
Suppresses expression of your thoughts, feelings and opinions	Allows you to express your thoughts, feelings and opinions
Brings about a distorted picture of yourself	Brings about a realistic picture of yourself
Results in self-doubt when you have done well	Results in self-affirmation/praise when you have done well
Creates feelings of worth being dependent on the way you are treated	Creates feelings of worth emanating from within, rather than solely dependent on the actions of others

ASSERTIVE EXPRESSION

Breaking the cycle also involves moving away from passive and aggressive reactions. With passive self-protection, the target, hounded by feelings of helplessness, retreats and becomes a pawn in the hands of any power-hungry bully. Being passive opens the door to being used by people and becoming a scapegoat. Being aggressive involves the target inflicting their pain on someone else in response to their own feelings of powerlessness. The target may also find themselves using passive-aggressive behaviour. This can take many forms, but generally is described as non-verbal aggression that manifests through negative behaviour (ie the person is angry with someone but, instead of saying so, gives angry looks or sulks etc).

Developing an assertive approach will be much more productive in dealing with bullies. This involves not being subservient (bowing down) or reactive (withdrawing, becoming quickly offended or having angry outbursts) but instead:

- Giving clear messages
- Not making communication personal
- Sticking to the point
- Expressing facts more than feelings
- Keeping things in the present
- Keeping the message simple, so as to be understood
- Having the right to make mistakes
- Explaining clearly what's needed, offering reasons and benefits
- Starting, changing and ending conversations
- Not allowing yourself to be used by others
- Offering alternative solutions
- Maintaining a sense of fairness
- Having the liberty to ask if unsure about something

- Using 'I' statements … 'I feel' rather than 'you make me feel'
- Addressing situations that bother you
- Refusing other people's requests if they are too demanding
- Questioning rules that don't make sense or appear unreasonable

In the early stages of bullying, the target tends to be intimidated by the bully and backs off or gives unclear messages. If, in fact, a more direct, assertive approach is used, in many cases, the bully is less likely to pursue the attack. John was being put down by a colleague at work and sought advice. The next time it happened, he made eye contact with the bully and gave the clear message: 'I don't appreciate it when you put me down and I'd like you to stop doing it.' It didn't happen again.

Tips for breaking the bullying cycle …
- Remember that *you* are in charge of your life, not the bully
- Hold on to the thought that the bully is more powerful in your *mind* than in *reality*
- Work at reducing stress levels, since stress blocks your ability to easily see alternatives
- Consider what you *can* change rather than focusing on what you *can't* change
- Walk away, physically, from abusive interactions, where possible
- Try not to justify your actions. If necessary, remain silent
- Express hurt and anger away from the bully, because bullies feed off reactions
- Look for solutions rather than focusing on the bullying and associated problems

- Develop a network of friends, as social isolation increases the risk of being bullied
- Remember that you *can* say 'no'
- Try to respond in a confident, assertive manner

REFLECTION

It's so easy to let the opinion of another person affect the opinion you hold of yourself, but it is vital to separate who you are from the negative words of others.

ACTION

Choosing to lay aside the negative completely, write down all the positive things about yourself: characteristics, gifts etc (eg intelligent, creative, thoughtful, sensitive, understanding, intuitive, good administrator, and so on).

PRAYER

I invite you to pray with me:

Dear God, You say that I am 'fearfully and wonderfully made' (Psa. 139:14). Help me to see myself in the way that You see me, rather than make judgments according to the words and actions of others. Amen.

CHAPTER 11

CHANGING STYLES
OF RELATING

When we are no longer able to change a situation, we are challenged
to change ourselves.

Victor Frankl[1]

LOOKING AT YOURSELF DIFFERENTLY

Any kind of abuse models unhealthy styles of relating. The way
we see ourselves and other people affects how we relate.

On the whole:

- Bullies see themselves as *above* others
- Targets see themselves as *subject* to others

In both cases, the relationship with the other person is not on
an equal basis. The bully needs to be 'top dog' and the target gives
in to being the 'underdog'. This imbalance keeps the bullying
cycle in operation and needs to change. Some may argue that
the bully *is* in a strong position (ie as an older sibling/child or
a manager at work etc) but it isn't age or rank that is the issue.

It's the fact that the target often perceives themselves as inferior or lacking in power which opens them up to the potential for intimidation. The target has the tendency to hold on to the belief that they have little control over their own lives: they see life as a fast-flowing stream and themselves as a piece of driftwood being swept along with the current.

It is liberating when the person can realise instead that life does not completely control them; they can make decisions which bring about a different outcome. It's important to know and believe that we all have the right to be treated with respect, decency and dignity, irrespective of age, position or role.

STYLE OF RELATING

How any one of us relates to another person has an impact and stimulates a response, be it positive or negative. A variety of tools are used to help people understand more about relational styles. One I've found particularly helpful is 'The Drama Triangle', which was first identified by Stephen B. Karpman, M.D., in 1968.[2]

THE DRAMA TRIANGLE

The Drama Triangle uses the concept of three roles:
- Victim
- Persecutor
- Rescuer

We all have the potential to take on these roles in different situations. When we act in one position it can stimulate an unhelpful response from someone else operating in one of the other roles.

THE DRAMA TRIANGLE
© Stephen B. Karpman, M.D.

Persecutor   Rescuer

Victim

Victim: assumes a position of *vulnerability* – accepts the role, feels helpless and does not take responsibility for self

Persecutor: assumes a position of *power* – intimidates, pressurises and persecutes the victim

Rescuer: assumes a position of *false responsibility* – gives the outward appearance of intervening but in a way that is not productive for the victim

Note: the 'victim role' is not the same as being a victim of a wrong action/crime and the 'rescuer role' is not the same as rescuing someone out of necessity in an emergency.

The Drama Triangle is an indirect form of communication and is self-focused, in as much as it is about the meeting of one's own psychological needs. The target often finds themselves in the position of the 'victim' and the bully in the position of the 'persecutor'. When relating healthily people aim to stay off the triangle, that is, their responses are neutral (ie 'I feel sad when this happens' rather than 'You're the one who makes me sad' – persecutor; or 'It's my fault I'm sad because I'm such a wimp' – victim). Staying off the Drama Triangle also means not using passive-aggressive behaviour. Passive-aggressive behaviour is not communicating honestly when you feel upset, annoyed, irritated or disappointed but rather, bottling the feelings up and closing down verbally; giving angry looks; being ambiguous, cryptic, unclear or obstructive; sulking, shutting people out, making excuses and expecting people to guess how you feel.

The following offers some insights as to how to tell whether you are on the Drama Triangle.

THE VICTIM ROLE

- Believing that others have the power to make you feel good or bad
- Expecting others to 'take care' of you rather than taking care of yourself
- Discounting your own value and allowing others to criticise you
- Letting someone else solve your problems when you have the ability to solve your own
- Needing love and attention through being rescued or cared for by others, thus actively or passively encouraging others to victimise you
- Not standing up for yourself or setting clear boundaries
- Expecting other people to guess how you feel rather than communicating your needs and feelings
- Easily feeling discounted, hurt, ignored, abused or taken advantage of
- Seeing other people as being responsible for your wellbeing

- Having a bias towards thinking: 'Why does it always happen to me?'; 'I'm not as valued'; 'People don't care'

THE PERSECUTOR ROLE
- Criticising others without understanding the reasons behind their actions
- Elevating your feelings at the expense of the other person
- Justifying your actions and criticism of others
- Conveying messages that say to someone else: 'I am better than you'; 'I have power over you'; 'You're no good'
- Persecuting others in order to avoid being a victim
- Being verbally, emotionally or physically abusive
- Coming across as an overly critical parent
- Having a bias towards using wording such as: 'You always …'; 'You never …'; 'You did what!'; 'If it wasn't for you ...'

THE RESCUER ROLE
- Tendency to be over-involved with someone else's feelings
- Taking personal choice and responsibility away from them
- Overprotecting and advising others, denying them the opportunity to seek solutions for themselves
- Feeling more responsible for others than for yourself
- Helping other people to distract yourself from facing/handling your own problems
- Gaining a personal sense of value through 'caring' for others
- Having a bias towards using wording such as: 'I'll sort it out for you'; 'You poor thing!'

One of the risks for the target is that not only do they step on to the Drama Triangle in their relationships with other people, but they also take on both victim and persecutor roles towards themselves. Their self-destructive beliefs become echoes of the words spoken negatively by others. They hold on to the pain, either feeling helpless and acting as a victim, or condemning themselves, becoming their own bully.

STEPPING OFF THE DRAMA TRIANGLE

How do we step off the Drama Triangle? By not acting in any of these roles but by staying neutral instead. Stepping off involves becoming aware of how the actions and words of other people trigger certain responses in us – some of which are unhelpful.

Leaving the victim role involves:
- Changing your own behaviour
- Focusing on clear problem-solving
- Setting clear boundaries
- Associating yourself with people who are mutually supportive
- Holding on to the rights you have as a human being, such as respect, being heard etc
- Endeavouring to recognise persecutor/rescuer roles operating in others
- Communicating your needs, likes and dislikes openly, but kindly
- Appreciating what you have, rather than dwelling on what you don't have
- Walking away from control and manipulation
- Taking initiative as opposed to expecting others to lead you

Leaving the persecutor role involves:
- Taking personal responsibility rather than blaming others
- Owning your emotions rather than projecting them on to others
- Finding a safe place and means of expressing anger and frustration
- Not punishing people in order to feel better
- Not excluding others
- Listening to your needs and the needs of others

Leaving the rescuer role involves:
- Letting others take responsibility for themselves
- Ensuring that your life consists of a balance of caring for others and yourself
- Allowing others to make personal choices
- Encouraging other people to do things for themselves rather than doing it for them
- Finding ways to feel affirmed other than through rescuing people
- Finding a balance of people to whom you relate, not just those who appear vulnerable

BODY LANGUAGE

Body language is powerful! It is said that over 80% of communication is non-verbal. Hence the way people walk, talk and hold themselves affects how they are perceived and treated by others. Posture, gestures, appearance, touch, tone of voice, face and eyes are all used in different forms of communication.

Body language often used	
Target:	**Bully:**
Passive stance, hunched shoulders	Aggressive stance, intrusive body language
Evidence of fear, sadness, submission or shock in the face	Peering over the top of glasses; looking down at the person
Smile is rather apprehensive	Smile is somewhat cocky
Reservation in the voice	Confidence, persuasion or anger in the voice
Movements which indicate submission, such as backing off or shuffling	Pointing, making a fist, pounding the desk and tapping fingers
Avoidance of eye contact (bullies tend to perceive lack of eye contact as a hidden agenda or lack of respect)	Glaring, narrowing, rolling or widened eyes indicating intimidation or disapproval
Fidgeting, looking anxious, carrying out nervous habits	Arms crossed over chest (being closed to what the other person is saying)
'Freezing' when the bully approaches or starts to speak to you	Interrupting or turning away before the target has finished speaking

Targets can help to reduce the effectiveness of bullying by developing a positive body language, such as:
- Being neither passive nor aggressive, but relaxed and genuine
- Not giving out messages that they are vulnerable or defensive
- Maintaining eye contact and expressing kindness and fairness through the eyes
- Turning towards the person who is speaking, indicating full attention

- Making sure that the smile is relaxed and sincere
- Standing up straight and feeling good about themselves
- Not giving the impression of nervousness by fiddling with hands/hair etc.
- Keeping a comfortable distance but choosing not to back away or shuffle
- Maintaining a strong, clear voice.

PAUSE FOR THOUGHT ...

Are you aware of your body language and facial expressions? Perhaps you'd like to practise one or two of the above with someone you trust. This can help you to 'do it for real' at a later point.

SETTING BOUNDARIES

The key to breaking the Bullying Cycle is recognising what draws the target into the bully's destructive web and responding differently. Bullying is maintained partly by compliance; hence if the target does not comply, the bully's actions will have limited effect. As the target learns to set boundaries, be more assertive and no longer give the bully what they want, the bully's attempts to control, manipulate and intimidate will be weakened.

Those who are vulnerable to repetitive bullying may have had inadequate role modelling and learning experiences about boundaries in childhood.

> Boundaries are guidelines, rules or limits that a person creates to identify for themselves what are reasonable, safe and permissible ways for other people to behave around them and how they will respond when someone steps outside those limits ... When our own

personal boundaries are routinely broken, the message we learn is that our own needs and feelings don't count – we are required to accept how others treat us without question. As we grow into adults, these lessons can become our way of life. We often feel taken advantage of, used or that our desires are unimportant. We become frustrated and angry that our boundaries are violated yet we are unable to express what, exactly, our boundaries are. Constant yielding to a parent, sibling or relative becomes second nature. We lose our own sense of self and often find ourselves in unhappy relationships, jobs and life situations. The early lessons that our feelings, views and opinions don't count continue to dominate our lives, sometimes subconsciously.[3]

In order to set boundaries, a person needs to have knowledge of what boundaries are, together with the confidence and assertiveness to set them. A part of my research for this book involved compiling a questionnaire. One of the questions I asked was: *'How has bullying affected your relationship with others?'* Interestingly, most people replied that bullying had affected confidence, relationship with people, and boundaries. One person said: *'I have no boundaries and let people do what they want because I feel it is only me and I don't really matter.'*

Boundary tips …
- Communicate that you expect to be treated with respect, as you treat others
- Take your own needs into account, as well as those of others, when considering a response
- When you say 'No', stick to it; don't keep changing your mind
- Remember that someone endeavouring to make you feel guilty

is no reason to say 'Yes'
- Make it clear that you are capable of making your own decisions
- Communicate directly rather than through behaviour or implication

Becoming aware of body language and learning to relate in a different way are good ways to resist bullying. We cannot stop bullying from happening completely because, sadly, it is a part of human nature. However we can develop skills which reduce the effectiveness of bullying and which challenge the bullying behaviour.

REFLECTION
'Tears are words the heart can't express.' (unknown)

ACTION
At the time you are crying, it can be difficult to know what the tears represent. It can sometimes be easier to think about what your tears represented when you are in a calmer place. If your tears had words, what might they say? 'I am ... I feel ... I fear ...?'

PRAYER
I invite you to pray with me:
Dear God, the psalmist says of You: 'You keep track of all my sorrows. You have collected all my tears in your bottle. You have recorded each one in your book' (Psa. 56:8, NLT). Thank You for caring. Amen.

CHAPTER 12

RECOVERING FROM THE TRAUMA

Understanding is the first step to acceptance, and only with acceptance can there be recovery.

J.K. Rowling[1]

PHYSICAL RESTORATION

If you've gone through the trauma of being bullied, you will inevitably have struggled not only with upsetting emotions, frightening memories, a sense of danger and the inability to trust other people, but also reactions for which your body has paid a price.

COMBATING STRESS

Bullying brings with it much stress. Stress that continues without relief can lead to a condition called 'distress' – a negative stress reaction. It's all too easy to concentrate on the emotional healing needed and forget that the body too is in need of repair.

People do not always realise that the symptoms they are experiencing relate directly to stress from the bullying – especially when those symptoms are physical, such as infections, lack of energy, muscle weakness, hormone imbalances, glandular fever and so on. The body is, in fact, harmed under stress. It has a 'fight or flight' mechanism which is designed to operate when imminent danger is probable or perceived. Certain hormones (like adrenalin and cortisol) are released, speeding up the heart rate, slowing digestion, shunting blood flow to major muscle groups, and changing various autonomic nervous functions, so giving the body a burst of energy and strength to fight or run from the danger.

When the perceived threat is gone, all systems are designed to return to normal function by the body relaxing. However, in situations like bullying, neither response (fight or flight) is actually appropriate. Rather than being activated only for a short time, the stress response is kept going for longer periods, and the 'switch off' doesn't happen sufficiently to allow the body to recover. The body ends up in a semi-permanent reactive state. The over-release of chemicals into the body becomes toxic to the system, and the body's physical, emotional and mental reserves begin to run dry, causing damage. There are many symptoms, not least fatigue and suppression of the immune system.

Tips for recovery ...
- Look at ways to reduce general stress levels
- Endeavour to keep life simple for a while (not juggling too much)
- Take rest when needed (the effects of bullying are exhausting)
- Relax your body (exercise, swim, massage, rest etc)
- Make sure you eat a healthy, balanced diet (with plenty of fresh

fruit, vegetables, unprocessed foods, wholegrains and protein)
- Consider taking vitamin and mineral supplements (stress can deplete the body of necessary supplies)

EMOTIONAL HEALING

Bullying erodes a person's sense of self and it can take years for the shattered, demoralised person to be built into a secure, confident individual. The target has lived with continuous negative input which seriously affects the view of both themselves and the world. It makes you wonder how anyone can heal from the emotional battering. We all have our own way of healing but talking about what has happened, preferably in a therapeutic setting, and being allowed to grieve is an important part of the process, as is coming to the conclusion that the bullying is not your fault and does not make you a bad person.

Some of the damage is only undone as the opposite is encountered: where, instead of ridicule and exclusion there is acceptance, affirmation and inclusion.

Gill speaks of her experiences:

The bullying I endured for several years at work on top of childhood bullying stripped the core of me away and changed me. Not only did it result in crushing pain but each time I was ridiculed or put down I went that little further into myself; became shyer. The constant criticism made me suspicious and, dare I say, even critical of others and I didn't like who I had become. Through therapy I began to make sense of my broken world and I faced the pain and the defences I had put up. With skilled help my fragmented self become more whole but equally important was the love and affirmation from others. The ongoing encouragement of one or two faithful people, without being perpetually shamed, enabled my feelings of unworthiness to lessen. Their approval and inclusion of me, even when I still struggled to know whether I was 'good' or 'bad', helped me to have faith in life once more and feel less fearful of others.

People recovering from the effects of bullying require understanding, warmth, compassion, validation, acceptance, respect, empathy, encouragement and support. They need to be free from pressure, to be in a safe environment, to feel in control of their circumstances and to have time to work through their pain and come to terms with what has happened.

RESTORING WORTH

Bullying ravages a person's sense of worth. Recovering from its effects involves restoring that which has been so cruelly stolen. Other people can affirm and speak positives, but the most important input is, in fact, from the target themselves. The healing needed is far deeper than the soothing, palliative and corrective words of others. If you do not learn to affirm yourself then the words of others are too easily glossed over.

Michel de Montaigne (1533–1592), one of the most influential writers of the French Renaissance, once said: 'I do not care so much what I am to others as I care what I am to myself.' We all need to be less concerned about what other people think of us and more vigilant about what we think of ourselves. Who are we to think badly of ourselves if we are made in the image of the Creator of the universe who loves us unconditionally? 'The LORD appeared to us in the past, saying: "I have loved you with an everlasting love; I have drawn you with loving-kindness"' (Jer. 31:3).

The actions of others may hurt us, but ultimately what counts is the fact that God is for us. The apostle Paul, in his letter to the Romans, encourages us: 'If God is for us, who can be against us?' (Rom. 8:31b).

IDENTIFYING SAFE PEOPLE

Bullies bring with them deceit, cover-ups, lack of honesty, inconsistency, unpredictability and huge variations in temperament. Both trust and a sense of security are shattered in the target, and it takes time to feel safe again. To help prevent further damage, it's important for the already wounded person to learn how to identify safe people and to avoid, where possible, too much interaction with those who bring mixed messages and behave in harmful ways. Interacting with people who are consistent, keep their word, remain confidential, and who are non-reactive and predictable, helps to rebuild trust and confidence.

PAUSE FOR THOUGHT ...

Amongst the people you know, who would you describe as a) a safe person and b) an unsafe person? Do you know what it is about the 'unsafe' person that makes you wary? Perhaps the lists below will help you to pinpoint significant areas.

Drs Henry Cloud and John Townsend list traits of 'unsafe' people in their book entitled *Safe People*.

PERSONAL TRAITS OF UNSAFE PEOPLE[2]

- Unsafe people think they 'have it all together' instead of admitting their weaknesses
- Unsafe people are religious instead of spiritual
- Unsafe people are defensive instead of open to feedback
- Unsafe people are self-righteous instead of humble
- Unsafe people only apologise instead of changing their behaviour
- Unsafe people avoid working on their problems instead of dealing with them
- Unsafe people demand trust instead of earning it
- Unsafe people believe they are perfect instead of admitting their faults
- Unsafe people blame others instead of taking responsibility
- Unsafe people lie instead of telling the truth
- Unsafe people are stagnant instead of growing

INTERPERSONAL TRAITS OF UNSAFE PEOPLE[3]

- Unsafe people avoid closeness instead of connecting
- Unsafe people are only concerned about 'I' instead of 'we'
- Unsafe people resist freedom instead of encouraging it
- Unsafe people flatter us instead of confronting us
- Unsafe people condemn us instead of forgiving us
- Unsafe people stay in parent/child roles instead of relating as equals
- Unsafe people are unstable over time instead of being consistent
- Unsafe people are a negative influence on us, rather than a positive one
- Unsafe people gossip instead of keeping secrets

Tips for recovery ...

- Commit to a recovery process: therapy, counselling, prayer ministry etc
- Spend time with people who are 'safe' and will build you up rather than tear you down
- Keep developing life skills, such as assertiveness, boundary setting, communication etc
- Maintain outside interests and work at having meaning, purpose and direction in your life
- Begin to set your own terms rather than always live by those of other people
- Seek an outside perspective/alternative point of view to situations that overwhelm
- Work on changing the way you handle situations, avoiding extreme reactions
- Endeavour to tackle one problem at a time in your life, rather than everything all at once
- Consider your own stress-induced thoughts, feelings and behaviours
- Develop your sense of humour and try to include something enjoyable each day
- Share your feelings with a trusted friend; don't bottle emotions up
- Challenge your own negative thinking, which only leads to low feelings
- Relax your mind (build in time and an activity free from 'thinking', such as creativity, listening to music etc)

SPIRITUAL FREEDOM

Bullying is not in God's plan and goes against His very nature and His desire for us as His children. In the Old Testament it says:

> There are six things the LORD hates, seven that are detestable to him: haughty eyes, a lying tongue, hands that shed innocent blood, a heart that devises wicked schemes, feet that are quick to rush into evil, a false witness who pours out lies and a man who stirs up dissention among brothers (Prov. 6:16–19).

In the New Testament, the apostle Paul states clearly the attitudes we should hold towards others:

> Let everything you say be good and helpful, so that your words will be an encouragement to those who hear them (Eph. 4:29, NLT).

If you've been bullied it's important to remind yourself that this was never God's intention for you and it's also *not your fault*. Rather than blame God, try to recognise that we live in a fallen world where, sadly, people say and do very harmful things. The wounds will run deep and will take time to heal, and spiritual help may be needed in the recovery process. This is where prayer ministry, as well as Christian counselling, has helped many people. Below is a prayer you can pray. It is not a formula, but rather a model of how to pray.

PRAYER

Lord Jesus, You knew what it was to suffer cruelty and bullying during Your final days on earth. I ask You, as the Prince of Peace, to bring peace to me. May I know that You are with me and may I feel Your deep love for me.

I place Your cross between me and those who have bullied me and I ask that through the power of Your blood You cut me free from the destructive words spoken. Where the words or images have caused disharmony, disease or disorder within me, please restore Your harmony, ease and order into my life. Set me free from, and heal, the pain, trauma, shock, fear, terror and shame which have resulted from the bullying.

Thank You that You rejoice over me with singing (Zeph. 3:17).

Pour in Your love and grace and, by the power of the Holy Spirit, remove any traumatic memory stored in the cells of my mind and body. Bring Your healing power into every area where my spirit has been crushed or broken, and restore health and vitality. May I receive Your promises, and learn to trust again. Thank You.

Amen.

Try to hold on to scriptural truths in the midst of the pain, such as Psalm 118:5–6 (NLT):

In my distress I prayed to the LORD,
  and the LORD answered me and set me free.

The LORD is for me, so I will have no fear.
  What can mere people do to me?

FORGIVENESS

Forgiveness is not easy, and when you have been wounded by someone it's difficult to understand why you should forgive them. 'Why should they be let off the hook?' you say to yourself. That's precisely why forgiveness is necessary: unforgiveness links us to the individual; forgiveness releases us from them. Forgiveness does not mean that your experience is being minimised or that what the bully did was right. It simply means that you let go of the responsibility of the consequences for the bully and separate yourself spiritually and emotionally. Forgiveness is not so much about releasing the bully but about you releasing yourself from the bully. The consequences of the bully's wrong actions do not belong to you, but to God, who deals with us all justly and fairly.

Whilst forgiveness is necessary and an essential part of healing, you may not yet be ready to start the journey. An important first step will be to take courage and ask God to help you. Forgiveness tends to come in layers. In the moment, we forgive in the way we can. As we process what has happened, we find that we are more able to forgive – and in a deeper way. If you simply wait until you *feel* like forgiving, you will wait forever.

PRAYER

Heavenly Father, You know the bullying I have been through. It both hurts me and has affected my life. I ask that You heal me. Please help me to forgive those who have hurt me. Although it is hard, with Your enabling I take the first steps to forgive _____ for _____ and all their acts of unkindness. I hand them over to You to deal with. Cut me free from them, renew my mind to think positively about life and about myself, and deliver me from oppression by the enemy. I ask this in Jesus' name. Amen.

Equally important as forgiving the bully is forgiving yourself. It's all too easy to hold on to unforgiveness towards yourself, perhaps thinking that you have 'allowed' yourself to be bullied and believing that it happened, in part, because you are a 'bad' person. As and when you feel ready to work through forgiveness, you may find it helpful to ask yourself:

- Do I want to get my own back on the bully?
- Do I feel that the bully should suffer in the same way?
- Am I holding on to bitterness and resentment?
- Am I resentful towards those who knew something of the bullying and didn't help?
- Am I able to forgive myself for not having recognised the problem earlier?
- Am I able to forgive myself for 'allowing' the bullying to continue?

Feeling angry for the way you have been treated is normal. However, be careful not to go down the road of bitterness, lest you become like the bully in attitude.

What you can do:
- Recognise the spiritual dimension of bullying
- Put on the full armour of God each day (Eph. 6:10–18)
- Hand the bully over to God and ask Him to deal with the person
- Forgive the bully and those who have harmed you, let you down and not supported you
- Seek prayer ministry to deal with any spiritual roots to your bullying

MOVING FORWARD

As the wounds begin to heal, there comes a time when the person targeted begins to feel that they can now step out into new territory. Growing in boldness and courage happens as a person feels empowered. The meaning of being empowered is 'to enable or permit'. Empowering oneself is about overcoming and rising above negative situations; feeling in control rather than controlled. Since targets have been disempowered by bullying and often feel as if they live in a state of paralysis, empowerment is a significant part of their healing journey. Empowerment brings them the boldness, courage and tenacity to deal with situations. It's about feeling capable, able, competent and adequate; being able to embrace life, rather than shy away from it.

> Our lives are not determined by what happens to us, but by how we react to what happens; not by what life brings to us, but by the attitude we bring to life. A positive attitude causes a chain reaction of positive thoughts, events and outcomes. It is a catalyst, a spark that creates extraordinary results. (Anon)

You feel empowered when you …
- Break the silence about being bullied
- Find the courage to explain what has happened
- Express emotions in healthy ways
- Set clear boundaries
- Believe in your own abilities
- Engage in activities which give you a sense of purpose
- Set goals which you can and do achieve
- Find fulfilment in what you do
- Use your gifts and talents

- Make the most of opportunities
- Face and resolve conflict
- Discuss options and make choices

Being empowered is what enables you to say …
- 'I'm not standing for being bullied'
- 'I'm not going to let the effects ruin the rest of my life'
- 'I'm going to do whatever I can to bring it to an end or move away from this situation'
- 'I'm going to believe that I have rights and choices, rather than be powerless'

We have journeyed together along the rough and perilous road of understanding bullying; a journey which, at times, may have been both painful and enlightening. I hope that, whatever your reason for reading this book, you will have been helped – either personally or in your desire to help others. I pray that you will join me in tackling bullying and standing up for those whose lives have been shattered by its destructive stamp.

REFLECTION
Hold on to the belief that wherever you are on your journey of recovery from bullying, you will heal.

ACTION
Take the piece of paper on which you have recorded your thoughts about those who've hurt you. Turn the paper over and write:
1. What you have most gained through reading this book
2. A declaration for yourself about no longer being a victim,

but having power and strength through God who made you, formed you and loves you. You may like to keep the paper or you may find it helpful to destroy it.

Suggested declaration ...
Although I have been bullied and wounded by the actions of others, I declare that I am not a victim and will not live my life with a victim mentality. I am of worth and value. I have gifts and abilities and I do not deserve to be 'put down', bullied or shamed by another person.

PRAYER
I invite you to pray with me:
Dear God, You and only You know all that I have been through. I ask You to go on healing the wounds and to strengthen me to step out with boldness and courage in a new way. Help me, every day, to find the positives in life. Amen.

For information on Helena's writing and speaking visit: www.helenawilkinson.co.uk

NOTES

INTRODUCTION

1. According to Bullying UK's 2006 National Bullying Survey (the largest, most comprehensive survey of its kind at the time).
2. 'Bullying at Work: Guidelines for UNISON branches, stewards and safety representatives', www.unison.org.uk/acrobat/13375.pdf

CHAPTER 1

1. www.bullyonline.org Tim Field.
2. www.kickbully.com created by Dave Chapman.
3. E. Tattum and D. Tattum, *Social Education and Personal Development* (London: David Fulton, 1992).
4. http://thinkexist.com/quotes/carl_w._buechner/

CHAPTER 2

1. http://sites.google.com/site/swanezine/bully-quotes Perry Morgan.
2. N. Willard, M.S., J.D., *Educator's Guide to Cyberbullying, Cyberthreats & Sexting*, Center for Safe and Responsible Use of the Internet. http://www.csriu.org/cyberbully/documents/educatorsguide.pdf

CHAPTER 3

1. www.bullyonline.org Tim Field.
2. http://news.bbc.co.uk/1/hi/business/3563450.stm
3. www.acas.org.uk
4. http://www.workplacebullying.org/2011/05/04/npost/ Ray Williams.
5. http://www.workplacebullying.co.uk/aethesis.html 'Bullying in the Workplace – An acceptable cost?' Andy Ellis, Ruskin College, Oxford, UK.
6. www.kickbully.com created by Dave Chapman.
7. www.mediate.com//articles/eddyB1.cfm Bill Eddy, Mediate at Work.
8. www.bullyonline.org Tim Field.
9. www.bullyonline.org Tim Field.

CHAPTER 4
1. B.J. Lueders, from article entitled, 'Emotional and Verbal Abuse' (2002). www.BethLueders.com
   For full article see http://www.focushelps.ca/article/addictions-abuse/verbal-and-emotional-abuse/emotional-and-verbal-abuse
2. Lenore E. Walker, *The Battered Woman* (New York: Harper and Row, 1979). See http://en.wikipedia.org/wiki/Cycle_of_abuse
3. www.bethelcog.org/church/general-articles/gods-commandments/the-great-commandment

CHAPTER 5
1. R. Enroth, *Churches That Abuse* (Grand Rapids, MI: Zondervan, 1992).
2. J. VanVonderen, D. and J. Ryan, *Soul Repair: Rebuilding Your Spiritual Life* (Leicester: IVP, 2008), p.20.
3. D. Johnson and J. VanVonderen, *The Subtle Power of Spiritual Abuse: Recognising and Escaping Spiritual Manipulation and False Spiritual Authority Within the Church* (Grand Rapids, MI: Bethany House, 2005).
4. S. Hall, 'Spiritual Abuse', *Youthwork*, March 2003, pp.32-35.
5. Insights gained from D. Johnson and J. VanVonderen, *The Subtle Power of Spiritual Abuse: Recognising and Escaping Spiritual Manipulation and False Spiritual Authority Within the Church* (Grand Rapids, MI: Bethany House, 2005); Prince Y. Okeyan, *Manipulation, Domination & Control* (Eastbourne: Kingsway, 2000); S. R.Arterburn and J. Felton, *Toxic Faith* (Colorado Springs: Shaw Books, 1991,2001); K. Blue, *Healing Spiritual Abuse* (Downers Grove, IL: IVP,1993); Ronald N. Enroth, *Churches that Abuse* (Grand Rapids, MI: Zondervan, 1992).
6. J. O'Donohue, *Anam Cara: Spiritual Wisdom from the Celtic World* (London: Bantum Press, 1999), p.16.

CHAPTER 6
1. Eleanor Roosevelt (1884-1962), First Lady of the United States from 1933-45, during the four presidential terms of her husband, Franklin Delano Roosevelt.
2. G. Simon Jr. PhD., *In Sheep's Clothing: Understanding and Dealing with Manipulative People* (Little Rock: Parkhurst Brothers, 2010).
3. www.kickbully.com Concepts paraphrased by Helena Wilkinson.

CHAPTER 7

1. www.bullyonline.org Tim Field.
2. D. Olweus, *Bullying at School: What We Know and What We Can Do (Understanding Children's Worlds)* (Hoboken, NJ: Wiley-Blackwell, 1993).
3. C.M. Brodsky, *The Harassed Worker* (Lexington: Lexington Books, 1976).
4. S. Einarsen, H. Hoel, D. Zapf & C.L. Cooper (Eds.), *Bullying and Emotional Abuse in the Workplace: International Perspectives in Research and Practice* (London: Taylor and Francis, 2003 edition).
5. www.kickbully.com created by Dave Chapman. Concepts paraphrased by Helena Wilkinson.

CHAPTER 8

1. Jonatan Mårtensson, quoted in Joyce Meyer, *Living Beyond Your Feelings* (London: Hodder & Stoughton, 2011).
2. S. Allison, L. Roeger, and N. Reinfeld-Kirkman, 'Does school bullying affect adult health? Population survey of health-related quality of life and past victimisation', *Australian and New Zealand Journal of Psychiatry*, Vol. 43, 2009, pp.1163-1170.
   L. Roeger, S. Allison, R. Korossy-Horwood, K.A. Eckert and R.D.Goldney, 'Is a history of school bullying victimisation associated with adult suicidal ideation?: a South Australian population-based observational study', *Journal of Nervous and Mental Disease*, Vol. 198, 2010, pp.728-733.
3. www.bullyonline.org Tim Field.
4. www.fightcrime.org/reports/BullyingReport.pdf
5. http://www.sciencedaily.com/releases/2008/04/080422143529.htm
6. http://www.b-eat.co.uk/PressMediaInformation/PressReleases/ Bullyingandeatingdisorders
7. www.bullyonline.org Tim Field.
8. http://library.thinkquest.org/07aug/00117/bullyingconsequences.html
9. www.bullyoline.org Tim Field.
10. www.med.upenn.edu/ctsa/ptsd_symptoms.html, University of Pennsylvania, Department of Psychiatry, Penn Behavioral Health, Center for the Treatment and Study of Anxiety, (3535 Market Street, 6th Floor, Philadelphia, PA 19104).

11. Herman, J., *Trauma and Recovery; The aftermath of violence from domestic abuse to political terror* (New York: Basic Books, 1997).

CHAPTER 9

1. Benjamin Disraeli (1804–81), 1st Earl of Beaconsfield, a British statesman and writer. Of Jewish ancestry, he was baptised a Christian in 1817. His political essays and novels secured him an enduring place in English literature. Elected to Parliament in 1837, he grew into an exceptional, practical, and scathingly witty politician.
2. Harvey Forbes Fierstein (born June 6, 1952), American actor and playwright.

CHAPTER 10

1. Randy Harrison, American actor. http://www.brainyquote.com/quotes/authors/r/randy_harrison.html

CHAPTER 11

1. V. Frankl, *Man's Search for Meaning* (Rider, 1946). Austrian psychiatrist and psychotherapist (1905-1997).
2. S. B. Karpman, 'Fairy Tales and Script Drama Analysis' in *Transactional Analysis Bulletin* Vol. 7, April 1968, Carmel, No. 26, pp.39-40. See www.nancycarterlcsw.com/DramaTriangle.html
3. www.outofthefog.net/CommonNonBehaviors/Boundaries.html

CHAPTER 12

1. J.K. Rowling, British author http://thinkexist.com/quotes/with/keyword/recovery/
2. Dr H. Cloud and Dr J. Townsend, *Safe People* (Grand Rapids: Zondervan, 1995) pp.28-38.
3. Ibid., pp.41-58.

USEFUL RESOURCES

BOOKS

John Bevere, *Breaking Intimidation: How to Overcome Fear and Release the Gifts of God in Your Life* (Lake Mary, FL: Charisma House, 2007).

Harriet B. Braiker, Ph. D., *The Disease to Please: Curing the People-Pleasing Syndrome* (New York: McGraw-Hill Professional, 2002).

Harriet B. Braiker, Ph.D., *Who's Pulling Your Strings? How to Break the Cycle of Manipulation and Regain Control of Your Life* (New York: McGraw-Hill Professional, 2004).

David Emerald, *The Power of TED (The Empowerment Dynamic)* (Edinburgh: Polaris Publishing Group, 2 Rev Upd Edition, 2009).

Tim Field, *Bully in Sight, How to Predict, Resist, Challenge and Combat Workplace Bullying – Overcoming the Silence and Denial by Which Abuse Thrives* (Didcot, Oxon: Success Unlimited, 1996).

David Graves, *Fighting Back: How to Fight Bullying in the Workplace* (New York: McGraw-Hill Professional, 2002).

David Johnson and Jeff VanVonderen, *The Subtle Power of Spiritual Abuse: Recognising and Escaping Spiritual Manipulation and False Spiritual Authority Within the Church* (Grand Rapids, MI: Bethany House Publishers, Reprint Edition, 1995).

David Kinchin, *Post Traumatic Stress Disorder, The Invisible Injury* (Didcot, Oxon: Success Unlimited, 2004).

Gary Namie, Ph.D., and Ruth F. Namie, Ph.D., *The Bully-Free Workplace: Stop Jerks, Weasels, and Snakes from Killing Your Organization* (Hoboken, NJ: John Wiley & Sons, 2011).

Joe Navarro, with Marvin Karlins, Ph.D., *What Every BODY is Saying: An Ex-FBI Agent's Guide to Speed-reading People* (New York: HarperCollins Publishers, 2008).

Dawn Newman-Carlson, Arthur M. Horne and Christi L. Bartolomucci, *Bully Busters: A Teacher's Manual for Helping Bullies, Victims & Bystanders* (Champaign, IL: Research Press, 2003).

Aryanne Oade, *Managing Workplace Bullying: How to Identify, Respond to and Manage Bullying Behaviour in the Workplace* (Basingstoke: Palgrave Macmillan Ltd., 2010).

Gary Smalley, Greg Smalley and Michael Smalley, *The DNA of Relationships* (Carol Stream, IL: Tyndale House Publishers, Inc., 2007).

Manuel J. Smith, *When I say No, I feel Guilty: How to Cope, Using the Skills of Systematic Assertive Therapy* (New York: Bantam USA, reissue edition, 1975).

Keith Sullivan, *The Anti-Bullying Handbook* (Thousand Oaks, CA: Sage Publications Ltd., 2010).

Anne-Renee Testa, *The Bully in Your Relationship: Stop Emotional Abuse and Get the Love You Deserve* (New York: McGraw-Hill Contemporary, 2007).

Jeff VanVonderen, Dale Ryan and Juanita Ryan, *Soul Repair: Rebuilding Your Spiritual Life* (Westmont, IL: IVP USA, 2008).

Diane Zimberoff, *Breaking Free from the Victim Trap: Reclaiming Your Personal Power* (Issaquah, WA: Wellness Press, 2011).

WEBSITES

GENERAL
www.anti-bullyingalliance.org.uk
Anti-Bullying Alliance contains all the key information on where to get help for children, young people, their families and professionals.

www.beatbullying.org
Campaigns to shape attitudes and change behaviours around bullying and provides training for parents/carers and professionals.

www.bullyonline.org
The world's leading website on bullying in the workplace and related issues including stress, PTSD and bullying-related suicide.

www.bullying.co.uk
Bullying UK includes young people, parents, schools, workplace, teen boundaries and cyberbullying.

www.mind.org.uk
A useful site dealing with a number of issues including bullying. Visit online shop, leaflets.

www.internetsafetyzone.co.uk
Information for adults and young people on cyberbullying, self-harm, eating disorders, suicidal feelings and online sexual exploitation.

www.bullying.org
The purpose of this site is to prevent bullying in society through education and awareness.

CHILDREN AND YOUNG PEOPLE

www.childline.org.uk
Tel: 0800 1111
A service for children and young people which is available via phone, email, text, message board and one-to-one chats online.

www.bullybusters.org.uk/kids
Provides support for victims and their families. Information for children, teenagers and adults and includes a confidential freephone helpline 0800 169 6928.

www.kidscape.org.uk
Provides individuals and organisations with practical skills and resources necessary to keep children safe from harm.

www.safechild.org
Provides teacher training, parent education and community awareness in relation to bullying, and sexual, emotional and physical abuse.

www.cyh.com
A child and youth health site, including very helpful, practical advice for
children who are being bullied.

www.bbc.co.uk/health/physical_health/child_development/teen_bully.shtml
A useful site for young people and parents addressing the nature of
bullying and what to do.

CYBERBULLYING
www.chatdanger.com
A site all about the potential dangers of interactive services online like
chat, IM, online games, email and on mobiles.

www.stopcyberbullying.org
Includes information for different age groups of children, parents/carers,
educators and law enforcement agencies.

www.thinkuknow.co.uk
Well laid-out site aimed at children of different age groups. Includes
sections for parents/carers and teachers/trainers.

WORKPLACE BULLYING
www.kickbully.com
A very useful and comprehensive guide to fighting workplace bullies.

www.thepeoplebottomline.com
An excellent South African site on workplace violence, stress and
bullying.

www.acas.org.uk/index.aspx?articleid=797
A very useful downloadable PDF on bullying and harassment at work.

www.management-issues.com/2006/5/25/blog/the-real-effects-of-
workplace-bullying-.asp
A very useful site which looks at the nature and effects of workplace
bullying, as well as dealing with the bully.

RELATIONSHIP BULLYING

www.verbalabuse.com
This site is dedicated to the recognition and prevention of verbal abuse in homes, schools and workplaces.

www.shrink4men.wordpress.com
A site for men who are recovering from relationships with abusive women and for the non-abusive family and friends who love them.

SPIRITUAL BULLYING

www.spiritualabuse.com
Resources for recovery from spiritual abuse.

www.balmnet.co.uk/burnout.htm
A resource for bullied ministers, but applicable to others damaged in a church setting.

www.difficultrelationships.com/2009/02/09/ten-signs-of-spiritual-abuse/
An excellent article stating ten signs of the presence of spiritual abuse, some of which are often not included in other resources

RECOVERY

http://helpguide.org/mental/emotional_psychological_trauma.htm
A very useful and practical site which addresses symptoms, treatment and recovery from trauma.

www.counselling-directory.org.uk
A useful site which covers many relevant subjects and also offers a directory of counsellors and psychotherapists who are registered with a recognised professional body.

National Distributors

UK: (and countries not listed below)

CWR, Waverley Abbey House, Waverley Lane, Farnham, Surrey GU9 8EP.
Tel: (01252) 784700 Outside UK (44) 1252 784700 Email: mail@cwr.org.uk

AUSTRALIA: KI Entertainment, Unit 21 317-321 Woodpark Road, Smithfield, New South Wales 2164.
Tel: 1 800 850 777 Fax: 02 9604 3699 Email: sales@kientertainment.com.au

CANADA: David C Cook Distribution Canada, PO Box 98, 55 Woodslee Avenue, Paris, Ontario N3L 3E5.
Tel: 1800 263 2664 Email: sandi.swanson@davidccook.ca

GHANA: Challenge Enterprises of Ghana, PO Box 5723, Accra.
Tel: (021) 222437/223249 Fax: (021) 226227 Email: ceg@africaonline.com.gh

HONG KONG: Cross Communications Ltd, 1/F, 562A Nathan Road, Kowloon.
Tel: 2780 1188 Fax: 2770 6229 Email: cross@crosshk.com

INDIA: Crystal Communications, 10-3-18/4/1, East Marredpalli, Secunderabad – 500026,
Andhra Pradesh. Tel/Fax: (040) 27737145 Email: crystal_edwj@rediffmail.com

KENYA: Keswick Books and Gifts Ltd, PO Box 10242-00400, Nairobi.
Tel: (020) 2226047/312639 Email: sales.keswick@africaonline.co.ke

MALAYSIA: Canaanland, No. 25 Jalan PJU 1A/41B, NZX Commercial Centre, Ara Jaya, 47301
Petaling Jaya, Selangor. Tel: (03) 7885 0540/1/2 Fax: (03) 7885 0545 Email: info@canaanland.com.my

Salvation Publishing & Distribution Sdn Bhd, 23 Jalan SS 2/64, 47300 Petaling Jaya, Selangor.
Tel: (03) 78766411/78766797 Fax: (03) 78757066/78756360 Email: info@salvationbookcentre.com

NEW ZEALAND: KI Entertainment, Unit 21 317-321 Woodpark Road, Smithfield, New South Wales
2164, Australia. Tel: 0 800 850 777 Fax: +612 9604 3699 Email: sales@kientertainment.com.au

NIGERIA: FBFM, Helen Baugh House, 96 St Finbarr's College Road, Akoka, Lagos.
Tel: (01) 7747429/4700218/825775/827264 Email: fbfm_1@yahoo.com

PHILIPPINES: OMF Literature Inc, 776 Boni Avenue, Mandaluyong City.
Tel: (02) 531 2183 Fax: (02) 531 1960 Email: gloadlaon@omflit.com

SINGAPORE: Alby Commercial Enterprises Pte Ltd, 95 Kallang Avenue #04-00, AIS Industrial
Building, 339420. Tel: (65) 629 27238 Fax: (65) 629 27235 Email: marketing@alby.com.sg

SOUTH AFRICA: Struik Christian Media, 1st Floor, Wembley Square II, Solan Street, Gardens, Cape
Town 8001. Tel: +27 (0) 23 460 5400 Fax: +27 (0) 21 461 7662 Email: info@struikchristianmedia.co.za

SRI LANKA: Christombu Publications (Pvt) Ltd, Bartleet House, 65 Braybrooke Place, Colombo 2.
Tel: (9411) 2421073/2447665 Email: christombupublications@gmail.com

USA: David C Cook Distribution Canada, PO Box 98, 55 Woodslee Avenue, Paris, Ontario N3L 3E5,
Canada. Tel: 1800 263 2664 Email: sandi.swanson@davidccook.ca

Courses and seminars

Publishing and new media

Conference facilities

Transforming lives

CWR's vision is to enable people to experience personal transformation through applying God's Word to their lives and relationships.

Our Bible-based training and resources help people around the world to:
• Grow in their walk with God
• Understand and apply Scripture to their lives
• Resource themselves and their church
• Develop pastoral care and counselling skills
• Train for leadership
• Strengthen relationships, marriage and family life and much more.

Our insightful writers provide daily Bible-reading notes and other resources for all ages, and our experienced course designers and presenters have gained an international reputation for excellence and effectiveness.

CWR's Training and Conference Centre in Surrey, England, provides excellent facilities in an idyllic setting – ideal for both learning and spiritual refreshment.

 CWR Applying God's Word
to everyday life and relationships

CWR, Waverley Abbey House,
Waverley Lane, Farnham,
Surrey GU9 8EP, UK

Telephone: +44 (0)1252 784700
Email: info@cwr.org.uk
Website: www.cwr.org.uk

Registered Charity No 294387
Company Registration No 1990308

Waverley Abbey Insight Pamphlets

These handy pamphlets contain key practical insights on various issues taken from our *Waverley Abbey Insight Series* of books. Based on our proven counselling courses, these short guides will equip you to understand and address problems effectively. Packs of 10 – always keep them handy for helping sufferers or their friends/relatives.

A Brief Insight into Stress
ISBN: 978-1-85345-608-4

A Brief Insight into Depression
ISBN: 978-1-85345-609-1

A Brief Insight into Dementia
ISBN: 978-1-85345-610-7

A Brief Insight into Eating Disorders
ISBN: 978-1-85345-611-4

A Brief Insight into Addiction
ISBN: 978-1-85345-635-0

A Brief Insight into Anxiety
ISBN: 978-1-85345-641-1

A Brief Insight into Self-Esteem
ISBN: 978-1-85345-637-4

A Brief Insight into Bereavement
ISBN: 978-1-85345-639-8

8-panel pamphlets,
216x99mm, packs of 10

More in the *Waverley Abbey Insight Series*

Insight into Addiction
by Andre Radmall
ISBN: 978-1-85345-661-9

Insight into Anger
by Wendy Bray and Chris Ledger
ISBN: 978-1-85345-437-0

Insight into Anxiety
by Clare Blake and Chris Ledger
ISBN: 978-1-85345-662-6

Insight into Assertiveness
by Christine Orme and Chris Ledger
ISBN: 978-1-85345-539-1

Insight into Bereavement
by Wendy Bray and Diana Priest
ISBN: 978-1-85345-385-4

Insight Into Dementia
by Rosemary Hurtley
ISBN: 978-1-85345-561-2

Insight into Depression
by Chris Ledger and Wendy Bray
ISBN: 978-1-85345-538-4

Insight into Forgiveness
by Ron Kallmier and Sheila Jacobs
ISBN: 978-1-85345-491-2

Insight into Perfectionism
by Chris Ledger and Wendy Bray
ISBN: 978-1-85345-506-3

Insight into Self-esteem
by Chris Ledger and Wendy Bray
ISBN: 978-1-85345-663-3

**Insight into Helping Survivors
of Childhood Sexual Abuse**
by Wendy Bray and Heather Churchill
ISBN: 978-1-85345-692-3

Insight into Stress
by Beverley Shepherd
ISBN: 978-1-85345-790-6

For information on CWR's one-day Insight seminars visit www.cwr.org.uk/insightdays

For current prices visit www.cwr.org.uk/store
Available online or from a Christian bookshop